FAITH
in the Fast Lane
How NASCAR Found Jesus

Chad Bonham

Foreword by Michael McDowell
Afterword by Billy Mauldin

JUDSON PRESS
PUBLISHERS SINCE 1824

Join our mailing list for updates and special offers.
www.judsonpress.com/mailing_list.cfm

FAITH in the Fast Lane: How NASCAR Found Jesus

Cover and interior design by Wendy Ronga/Hampton Design Group.
www.hamptondesigngroup.com

Library of Congress Cataloging-in-Publication data
Cataloging-in-Publication Data available upon request.
Contact cip@judsonpress.com.

Printed in the U.S.A.
First Edition, 2014.

PART 1: Moonshine, Motors, and Ministry

PART 2: Faith in the Fast Lane

Foreword

There's nothing like racing. Ever since I rode my first BMX bike, I've been in love with the exhilarating feeling that comes from competing against other racers and competing against myself. From BMX, I graduated to dirt bikes, and by the time I was eight years old, I was racing go-karts.

Ironically, I was never that interested in NASCAR. My dream was to drive in the Indy Car Series and other open wheel circuits like the Champ Car World Series. But when I was finally given the opportunity to step into a stock car, I was hooked. That led me to the ARCA series and eventually to NASCAR where I compete today in both the Sprint Cup Series and the Nationwide Series.

It didn't take long for me to realize that NASCAR is the most difficult form of racing. NASCAR has the best cars and the most advanced technology. It's a daily challenge to prove to myself and to others that I have what it takes to make it in the most exciting racing series in the world.

That's not the only thing that makes NASCAR unique. Its fans are extremely passionate and knowledgeable. And they aren't just fans for a given race weekend. They are fans for life. Because of the energy they bring to the track, we as drivers find ourselves competing in a Super Bowl–sized atmosphere everywhere we go.

What I've come to love about NASCAR is its rich history and its longtime commitment to public expressions of faith and to the facilitation of ministry—to the NASCAR community and its fans. NASCAR is the only professional sport that takes the time to pray before every event. It's not something it *has* to do, but rather it's something NASCAR *chooses* to do. From top to bottom, there is a passion to maintain stock car racing's Christian roots.

That's also why I believe NASCAR fans will enjoy reading *Faith in the Fast Lane*. The stories about how the faith movement was birthed and how it grew over the decades are both inspiring and intriguing. Many of these stories have never been told before and highlight visionaries of the faith—people who worked diligently to impact the NASCAR community with a message of hope, peace, and love.

I believe that the NASCAR story is really *everyone's* story. There are 43 drivers who compete each weekend in auto racing's most popular series. But we're not superheroes. We're not any different from the average Joe (or Jane). We all face constant challenges at our jobs, within our families, and with our friendships.

The Bible guarantees that no one is going to be free from struggles. God doesn't promise us that our lives won't have trials and that we won't face difficulties. In fact, the opposite is often true for the follower of Christ. While we're here on Earth, we're not going to reach that euphoria of perfection until we get to heaven. But God does promise us never to leave us or forsake us. God also gives us the strength to make it through anything that comes our way.

As you allow God's promises to take hold in your life, you will begin to understand and embrace the calling the Lord has given to you and to all of us. That's the message of this book. I hope that you will be challenged as you read the stories of people who made a huge impact on the lives of countless others because they answered that call.

Sometimes we feel like the task is too daunting. We don't always believe that we can do it, or we think we're not the right person for the job. But God works through broken, imperfect people. God can start a fire with a tiny little spark. Let the stories within this book inspire you to go out into your world and become a difference maker.

—Michael McDowell
NASCAR Sprint Cup driver

Acknowledgments

On June 26, 2011, I had a conversation with my oldest son, Lance, who was seven years old at the time. We had just gotten home from church, and as we stood in the dining room, I asked him what he had learned earlier that morning.

"Behold! I am coming again!" he boldly said with his index finger triumphantly pointing toward the sky.

After a brief conversation about the second coming of Christ, Lance added this thought: "You know what's cool about heaven? We'll get to meet the disciples."

I replied how I'd like to meet the prophet Daniel. My son quickly responded to that statement with another question: "You know who else I want to meet?" He answered without giving me time to guess. "Dale Earnhardt."

For that very reason, I want to first dedicate this book to Lance, my oldest of three boys, who could name most of the drivers, their car numbers, and their primary sponsors by the time he was five years old. Of course, my wife, Amy, and my two younger boys, Cole and Quinn, are equal inspirations in my journey as a writer. I could not do any of this without their unconditional love and support.

Besides Lance (who will be ten when this book releases), I'd also like to acknowledge the influence that my father-in-law, Rodger Rice, had on this project. This might come as a surprise to him, but my love for NASCAR was refueled back in 2000 after I married his daughter. Every time we would visit his and Joyce's place in Choctaw, Oklahoma, discussions about the sport inevitably dominated the conversation. And if there was a race on, you could bet that's what we were watching. In fact, I can also thank Rodger for raising his daughter to enjoy NASCAR broadcasts as much as I do. That's made my fourteen-plus years of marriage a whole lot easier at times.

And whenever I write a book, I always have to acknowledge my mother, Betty, who went to be with the Lord not long after I finished this project. Her years of prayer and support, along with the creative influence of my father, Stan (who went to heaven eight years earlier), have been the strength of my life. I also thank my sisters, Rhonda Dilldine and Karla Partridge; their husbands, Dusty Dilldine and Denton Partridge; my sister-in-law, Tracy Bean; and my nieces, Elizabeth Dilldine, Madison Dilldine, and Morgan Bean. All of them have been a blessing in more ways than they'll ever know.

I also thank Rebecca Irwin-Diehl of Judson Press, who has been an immensely patient advocate for this book every step of the way. Without her support and the editorial staff's hard work, this project would have never seen the light of day.

Over the course of roughly five years I interviewed fifty people for this book (some before the book was actually conceived). The following is a list of those gracious subjects: Ashley Allgaier, Justin Allgaier, Bobby Allison, Trevor Bayne, Dale Beaver, Lonnie Clouse, Brad Daugherty, Patricia Driscoll, Joe Gibbs, David Gilliland, Amy Gordon, Tim Griffin, Bobby Hillin Jr., Crystal Hornish, Sam Hornish Jr., Ned Jarrett, Stephen Keller, Matt Kenseth, Parker Kligerman, Blake Koch, Bobby Labonte, Dr. Roger Marsh, Mark Martin, Billy Mauldin, Teri MacDonald-Cadieux, Eric McClure, Jami McDowell, Michael McDowell, Hershel McGriff, Bryant McMurray, Larry McReynolds, Casey Mears, Mike Metcalf, Norm Miller, Joe Nemechek, Phil Parsons, Terri Parsons, Kyle Petty, Richard Petty, Andy Petree, Dr. Jerry Punch, David Ragan, David Reutimann, Robert Richardson, Melanie Self, Morgan Shepherd,

Ricky Stenhouse Jr., Tony Stewart, Nick Terry, and Darrell Waltrip. I specifically want to point out the contributions that Richard Guy made to this project. Until I met Richard, I had some major holes in my timeline that involved the ministry of Brother Bill Frazier. Our phone conversation and his book *With God You're Always a Winner* were invaluable resources that made the third chapter possible. I was also blessed to receive commentary and editorial insight from NASCAR historian Buz McKim. It was an honor to have his wealth of knowledge at my disposal. I also want to recognize Dr. Roger Marsh, who took the time to review some of the chapters, along with Billy Mauldin, who blessed me immensely by writing a powerful afterword for this project, as well as Michael McDowell who graciously took the time to write the foreword.

Special thanks also go out to the folks who helped me make those connections along the way: Andy Hall, ESPN; Motor Racing Outreach; Raceway Ministries; Richard Petty Motorsports; LeAnne Howell, Corey Wynn, Roush Fenway Racing; Megan Englehart, SPEED; Chris Helein, Joe Gibbs Racing; Cindy Shepherd, Shepherd Racing Ventures; Jennifer Chapple, JTG Daugherty Racing; Emily McClure, Hefty Brand Racing; Lauren Emling, Turner Scott Motorsports; NASCAR Hall of Fame; Stacie Fandel, Ryan Barry, Michael Waltrip Racing; Phil Parsons Racing; Randy Usher, NEMCO Motorsports; DeAnna Condos, Interstate Batteries; David Hovis, Chip Wile, Michael Ribas, Penske Racing; Doug Barnette, Player Management International, Inc.; Mike Zizzo, Texas Motor Speedway; Kelly Hale, Kansas Speedway; Jeff Dennison, Breaking Limits; Mike Davis, JR Motorsports; Back2Back Ministries; R3 Motorsports; Armed Forces Foundation; and Shawn Meekhof, MacDonald Motorsports.

And finally, and certainly most importantly, I want to give the glory and honor to my Heavenly Father for blessing me with the opportunity to do what I love. This is a privilege that I will never take for granted.

Introduction

It's Sunday morning in America. Half of the country is attending some kind of church service. The other half is sleeping in or perhaps enjoying a brunch at the local dining nook. But on this Sunday, one of thirty-six that take place between February and November at various venues across the country, a remarkable sight is developing right off I-35, just north of Fort Worth at the gargantuan Texas Motor Speedway.

On this sunny but cool late-October Sabbath Day in 2009, fans are pouring into the 138,000-seat stadium in anticipation of NASCAR's Sprint Cup Series Dickies 500. Race reporters are scrambling to get the last-minute scoop. NASCAR officials are making sure the track is in perfect condition for the day's big race. Sportswriters file into the media center for a pre-race meal and work on pre-race stories leading up to the dropping of the green flag.

For the NASCAR faithful, attending a race on Sunday is almost like going to church. Stock car racing certainly can become a religious experience for those rabid fans who follow the sport on a weekly, if not daily, basis. Yet most of the people in the stands are unaware of what is happening in a theater-styled room connected to the media center.

Right before the drivers and crew chiefs are dismissed from the mandatory drivers' meeting—a time when NASCAR officials emphasize the importance of good, clean racing and discuss whatever hot topics need to be addressed—a tall, slender man in his early fifties is asked to take the microphone. The audience instinctively rises in concert. Hats are removed. Heads are bowed.

Tim Griffin is the man who has seemingly commanded the immediate attention and respect of this increasingly diverse group of elite drivers. Griffin, the now former Motor Racing Outreach (MRO) chaplain for NASCAR's premier racing series, takes the next minute or so to say a prayer over the drivers, the crews, the officials, and the fans. At the utterance of the prayer's closing "Amen," the packed room suddenly shifts from quiet reverence to noisy commotion. Many of the drivers and crew chiefs exit stage left through a secure doorway that leads back to the Sprint Cup garage area. But others stay put. Additional crew members, spouses, children, NASCAR officials, sponsor reps, and even a handful of media types quickly join the fray.

Once everyone finds a place to sit (or in some cases, a place to stand at the back or along the sides), Griffin welcomes everyone to chapel and then introduces the day's guest worship leader. Two choruses later and Griffin is front-and-center again, sharing a message based on the New Testament book of Hebrews. It's part of a series that started way back in February at the Daytona 500.

For the average onlooker, the scene is a study in cultural dichotomies. First of all, it's difficult enough just getting past the fact that legendary drivers such as Mark Martin and Bobby Labonte are sitting next to each other with other popular personalities such as Matt Kenseth and David Ragan dispersed throughout the crowd. Kurt Busch sits next to Sam Hornish Jr. and his wife, Crystal, who is holding their little blonde-haired girl, Addison. Busch is noticeably, if not excusably, distracted by the playfully adorable toddler.

Busch's presence highlights the other noticeable oddity. His uniform is covered in Miller Lite logos. Perusing the crowd, other humorous pictures from the advertising cornucopia develop. Budweiser and Jim Beam (no longer active in

NASCAR) are well-represented. Another curious visual can be found four rows from the back, where two guys with the Crown Royal entourage are sitting in the same row as a crew member from the Extenze team. (For those who don't watch much late-night cable television, Extenze is a "male enhancement" product that is regularly promoted by porn stars in innuendo-laden infomercials.) Both Crown Royal and Extenze have since discontinued sponsorship within NASCAR, but other adult-oriented products remain involved.

Clearly, this is not something likely to be seen in any other church service on any given Sunday morning, but it plainly underscores the unique nature of faith's place in the NASCAR workspace. A day earlier, a similar scene unfolded with a smaller group of drivers and crew members from the Nationwide Series. A day before that, an even smaller group from the Craftsman Truck Series gathered to worship.

Fast forward to the present day, and we'll find that the scene at any given Sunday race is not much different. Stephen Keller, who replaced Griffin as the Sprint Cup chaplain, now stands behind the podium. Many of the same drivers faithfully attend, while several new faces have emerged to fill the makeshift pews—rising stars such as Trevor Bayne, Michael McDowell, and Landon Cassill. Sponsors have also changed. Economic troubles have forced many to leave the sport, while other stalwarts such as Home Depot, Lowe's, and M&M's can still be spotted on fire suits, polo shirts, and jackets throughout the room. But for the most part, the NASCAR chapel service is a consistent element of the sport's routine and tradition.

So why do these men and women attend these Sunday meetings? The reasons vary widely from one person to the next. Some use the religious activity as a "lucky charm" of sorts, perhaps for a good race or maybe just to ensure safety. Others attend out of a sense of moral obligation. They grew up in church, so embracing chapel seems like the right thing to do. Some drivers use the time as an escape from the many demands that have been placed upon them over the previous couple of days.

It's hard to know exactly what percentage of the chapel attendees fits into each of these categories, but it's clear that a growing number of NASCAR racers and team members are, at some level, influenced by a deeper sense of belief or a yearning to draw closer to their Creator. While church is ingrained into their lifestyle, they have grown beyond the habitual nature of such a gathering and regularly come to worship, to fellowship with like-minded believers, and to glean life-impacting truths from the Bible. It's a luxury that they are unable to enjoy nearly ten months out of every year. NASCAR chapel services have quite literally become the home church for these nonstop travelers.

As the thirty-minute session ends, this private display is literally taken into the public square. Amid the pre-race pageantry, viewers attending the race or watching from the comfort their couch at home or in a sports bar somewhere observe a prayer (usually presented by a local minister or series chaplain) followed by the national anthem. During the prayer, drivers stand with their spouses, children, or significant others with hats removed and heads bowed. The vast majority of fans do likewise. In a day and age when public prayer is often considered an act of political incorrectness, no one seems to mind.

As the drivers prepare to enter their cars, two men divide themselves between the forty-three cars. They offer the opportunity for a quick, personal prayer. Most accept. A very small handful of these athletes politely nod as if to say, "Thanks, but no thanks."

Once the race starts, most, if not all, of the spiritual activity takes a back seat. In fact, there's quite a contrast that even the casual observer can discern. Fans loosen up with the consumption of each alcoholic beverage. Profane language is directed at the drivers they love to hate, while equally salty dialogue reverberates over radio communications between spotters, crew chiefs, and those aforementioned drivers. Cars get wrecked, the victims retaliate, and post-race confrontations spill over into the garage.

In essence, the NASCAR race day experience is a lot like real life. Some people get along. Some people don't. Drama happens, and sometimes it gets ugly. And often all of this occurs in places where spirituality and irreverence run congruently. Sure, there are strong measures of faith to be found here, but this is by no means a sanitized environment.

So how did this all come together? If that question is directed toward the NASCAR phenomenon, well, it certainly wasn't created overnight. It has steadily grown from its earliest days in the South, when stock car racing was nothing more than moonshine runners having some fun on the weekends, to modern times, when support in the United States is second only to the almighty National Football League.

The same can be said about the strong faith presence at all NASCAR events. Faith and stock car racing have always been linked at various stages of its growth and at various levels of support within the community. Men and women of faith have significantly impacted the sport in both highly visible and subtle ways.

This book is unlike any other written about NASCAR. It is partly historical and partly inspirational. It shares numerous anecdotes—some that have been repeated often, others that have never been heard before now—and gives fans a glimpse into NASCAR's inner workings as they specifically relate to matters of faith. Part 1 takes a look at how the Christian faith has been a part of stock car racing since before it was officially a sport, and part 2 gives specific examples of how the faith movement is active in today's NASCAR culture.

But ultimately, this book hopes to reveal to us a little about ourselves through the lens of the complicated yet strangely simple world of stock car racing. Just like those who are part of the NASCAR "family," we too wrestle with our own imperfections, hypocrisies, and impure motives, all the while doing our best to live out faith atop our own platforms. There's much to be learned as we explore *Faith in the Fast Lane*.

CHAPTER 1

Rise and Moonshine

There's no denying it. NASCAR was birthed out of the illicit moonshine-running business that ran especially hot during the 1930s and 1940s. This used to be the sport's dirty little secret that no one wanted to acknowledge publicly, but oh, how times have changed. Evidence of this can be found at the NASCAR Hall of Fame in Charlotte, North Carolina, where a liquor still is proudly displayed. It serves as a celebration of stock car racing's once-obscured past.

Bryant McMurray knows a little something about that past. He's been studying stock car racing and its unique culture since first attending an event in 1960. In fact, McMurray teaches multiple classes about NASCAR at the University of North Carolina at Charlotte.

"For forty years, NASCAR didn't want to be associated with moonshine because it was a negative thing," he says. "And then with this new generation that came along in the late '90s and 2000s, it became a cool thing to talk about. 'You did jail time for making moonshine and the president pardoned you? Cool!' NASCAR started to see what it had there."[1]

Sometimes it seems as if the production of this iconic hard liquor is as old as the rolling North Carolina hills. It's not, of course, but "white lightning," as moonshine is also commonly called, has long been a staple throughout Wilkes County, primarily in towns such as Wilkesboro and North Wilkesboro.

That area is also known for its heavy Scots-Irish population. The two facts are by no means a coincidence. The Scots-Irish are the descendants of Protestant dissenters from the Irish province of Ulster. Their ancestors had migrated to North America during the eighteenth and nineteenth centuries and populated New England before fanning out to Southern states such as Virginia, Georgia, Kentucky, Tennessee, South Carolina, and North Carolina.

The Scots-Irish and their moonshine-making kin developed a long-standing contentious relationship with the United States government as early as the 1790s, when Congress placed a heavy tax on whiskey to help repay debts from the American Revolutionary War. This resulted in the infamous Whiskey Rebellion, which garnered swift and strong attention from President George Washington.

Over the next hundred years or so, moonshine production became a way of survival for Southern farmers, and because of the burdensome taxes that sometimes made the product unprofitable when sold legally, the Scots-Irish and other distillers hid their activities within the forested hills and mountainous regions.

By the early 1900s, a perfect storm was brewing. The Prohibition movement had picked up steam throughout the mid- to late 1800s and came to a head in 1919 with the ratification of the Eighteenth Amendment to the United States Constitution. This new federal law prohibited "the manufacture, sale, or transportation of intoxicating liquors within, the importation thereof into, or the exportation thereof from the United States."

At first, the legislation led to an overall decline in alcohol consumption. But the moonshine business, which was already operating outside of the law, actually saw a significant uptick in demand. And then, the other hammer dropped.

On October 29, 1929, the U.S. stock market suddenly crashed. "Black Tuesday," as it is often called, set off a chain of economic events that sent the world economy into the Great Depression, which would last until roughly the mid-1940s. Prohibition became even more unpopular during this time. The two factors contributed greatly to a sharp rise in moonshine's popularity. The producers desperately needed to sell and distribute the illegal substance just to survive, while the consumers found temporary comfort in the product.

"It was very hard in the '30s because of the Depression," NASCAR historian Buz McKim says. "It was a rather poor area anyway even in the best of times. Most of them were just dirt farmers. Moonshine was an opportunity to make some decent money—not just in the production, but also in the transportation."[2]

It didn't matter much to the Scots-Irish if it was the best of times or the worst of times. This headstrong people group was especially averse to heavy-handed government involvement. They had migrated to the United States in search of religious freedom, and now they were dealing with a different kind of struggle.

"Hauling whiskey that they made was a God-given right," McMurray says. "The government came in and put a tax on something they made out in their fields or in their woods. That wasn't right in their eyes. It was highly debatable as to whether it was illegal to have whiskey. These people were staunch independent Scots-Irish people that didn't believe in a lot of government meddling in their business."[3]

By the time Prohibition was repealed with the 1933 passage of the Twenty-first Amendment, moonshine was a booming business. An all-out war had broken out between the moonshiners and the federal tax collectors from the Alcoholic Beverage Control—the "revenuers."

Also, a new factor had been introduced into this rich American history lesson: the modern automobile. The transportation of moonshine was never more efficient than during the time when these four-wheel roadsters became widely available to anyone who had the money to afford one. And for the moonshiner, it was a necessity that could make or break one's business. Having a fast car was also the difference between freedom and imprisonment, hence the battle of wits to see who could modify their vehicles for the highest levels of speed.

After a while, the fight for survival turned into a recreational activity of sorts. Outrunning the revenuers was a badge of honor for the moonshiners and their drivers. Needless to say, these modified cars became legendary throughout the South and caught the attention of racing promoters who were on the cutting edge of a new sport.

Bill France Sr. was one of the first luminaries to catch the vision. In 1934 France moved his family from Washington, DC to Daytona. In 1936 he participated in the first stock car race on the Daytona Beach Road Course. That same year, moonshine cars migrated to Daytona to get a piece of the action. When France officially took over the events in 1938, the presence of these shady drivers with sketchy business practices was already deemed a small price to pay for the exciting product that he and his cohorts were able to field.

"The moonshine actually had little to do with the sport," McMurray explains. "The moonshine was the product that they carried in the cars that were modified and fit the racing profile that France needed to run the show. If they had been carrying flour or sugar or corn or anything else, it would have been the same thing. But when you built a vehicle to carry moonshine, you had to have a car that was quicker than the revenuers or a car that would outmaneuver them. That car fell right into the category of what was needed for stock car racing."[4]

Whether it was running from the law or running for the thrill of it, the moonshiners were just doing what they'd always done— surviving. One prominent aspect of that culture was particularly ironic in nature. The people from the early twentieth-century South tended to have an unwavering commitment to religion.

"NASCAR came out of the South, and it came out of hard times, difficult times, poor economies," Motor Racing Outreach president Billy Mauldin explains. "People were looking for something to do. I think it's the same reason we had the religious revivals that corresponded almost at the same time, if you want to go back to the Brush Arbor revivals. NASCAR came out of a region where people were looking for hope. Owning an automobile was a sign that you were moving up in life. It was all woven together to create an atmosphere that led to a sport being born amongst a group of people that may not have called themselves believers but would all call themselves respecters of God."[5]

This was especially true for the Scots-Irish, whose presence in the region was a direct result of their desire to have religious freedom apart from the oppression their ancestors faced back in Ireland. Originally, these immigrants were deeply rooted in the Presbyterian tradition, but over time the Christian community expanded to include a majority of Baptists and Methodists.

"It's ironic, but it's true," McMurray says. "The moral fiber of the person who was running the whiskey is that he was a Christian and he would go to church on Sunday, either before the race or if the race wasn't in town. That's how people were raised. The race wouldn't start until two or three in the afternoon, and that would give the church crowd enough time to go to church and then come to the track."[6]

The history of the Scots-Irish has been well-chronicled by James Webb in his book *Born Fighting*. Likewise, Neal Thompson, in his book *Driving with the Devil*, masterfully told the story of how moonshiners were the driving force behind NASCAR's formation.

But while the strong connection between the Southern moonshiners (in particular the Scots-Irish) and the Christian faith was clearly there, that information has received little study and dissemination until recently. Part of the discovery came when the region began to slowly shed the self-imposed embarrassment attached to its infamous roots.

Terri Parsons was among those on the forefront of that culture-shifting process. Before her husband, Benny (former Cup champion and TV broadcaster), passed away in 2007, he left her a top-ten list of things that he wanted her to get done. The third thing on that list was to get the North Wilkesboro Speedway reopened. In order to accomplish that feat, she needed to get the local community excited about its racing heritage, even the parts that previously had been deemed unattractive.

"For a long time, if you said the word moonshine, it was a very taboo thing," Parsons says. "People didn't want to say anything about moonshine. I would tell people, 'Do you understand that this is how auto racing got started?' But here in Wilkes County, they thought the devil was going to get you if you talked about the moonshining that happened here."[7]

Parsons is somewhat of a historian on the subject herself. She grew up in the shadow of the sport's iconic Daytona International Superspeedway and went to high school with the daughters of legendary drivers Fireball Roberts and Smokey Yunick. Her marriage to Benny further engrained her into NASCAR's historic lore. Before moving to North Carolina, Parsons had also been the director of tourism for Daytona Beach and understood the value that racing brought to her hometown.

Convincing the local authorities to use Wilkes County's moonshine past as a catalyst for rebuilding the local track was not going to be easy. So she decided to come up with a more subtle approach. Parsons wanted to hold an event on her property that would bring the old revenuers and moonshiners for a special VIP event. But first she needed to get the support of the area's most famous moonshiner turned NASCAR driver, Junior Johnson.

"I met with Junior for breakfast at his place," Parsons recalls. "When I told him what I wanted to do, he just about spit his coffee across the table."

"Honey, they're gonna ride you on a rail right back to Florida for that," Johnson flatly responded.[8]

But the Hall of Famer eventually came around and gave Parsons some invaluable advice. She first needed to get the North Wilkesboro and Wilkesboro police chiefs to agree in writing that they wouldn't prosecute the moonshiners for anything that they said at the gathering. Johnson was skeptical that the revenuers would want to be involved, but he said that he would help Parsons in any way he could.

After reassuring the local officials that this was a celebration of history and not the promotion of the moonshine business, Parsons hosted the first "Moonshiners and Revenuers Reunion" during the fall of 2009. Roughly 250 people attended that first event, including current and past drivers, crew chiefs, engine builders, and team owners. Attendees were mesmerized by the stories that these stock car racing luminaries shared. Parsons would go on to host two more events in 2010 and 2011 before the aging, and in some cases the passing, of key participants made it difficult to continue.

But many untold stories were revealed during those reunions, and many misconceptions about the moonshine era were broken down. Parsons was especially surprised to learn that the majority of the moonshiners were strict nondrinkers, or "teetotalers," mostly due to their religious convictions.

The revenuers likewise were guided by biblical principles that included an uncanny sense of compassion toward the very people they were chasing down on a daily basis.

"When the revenuers would go to arrest a moonshiner, sometimes it was sad because there would be a wife with four kids hanging all over her and babies and no groceries in the cabinet," Parsons says. "So at one of our events, I asked the question 'Which one of you bought groceries and took them back to the wife?' They all looked around at each other and three of them put their hands up in the air."[9]

Passionate to a fault yet humble and quiet concerning matters of religion and service, the Southern moonshiners and revenuers paved the way not just for the impending creation of NASCAR, but also for the longstanding tradition of faith expression that would initially be hidden and much later placed squarely in the spotlight.

"NASCAR is not a slice of the United States," McMurray says. "They may like to say that, but NASCAR is a slice of the South with its moral values and religion that has continued right on since the founding of the country. It might not be as strict, and it may not be as well-practiced, but the religion of the folks in NASCAR, especially the fans, is just as strong as it ever was."[10]

NOTES
1. Bryant McMurray, interview with the author, September 17, 2012.
2. Buz McKim, interview with the author, January 31, 2012.
3. Bryant McMurray, interview with the author, September 17, 2012.
4. Ibid.
5. Billy Mauldin, interview with the author, December 5, 2011.
6. Bryant McMurray, interview with the author, September 17, 2012.
7. Terri Parsons, interview with the author, March 8, 2012.
8. Ibid.
9. Ibid.
10. Bryant McMurray, interview with the author, September 17, 2012.

CHAPTER 2

Glimpses of Glory

Bill France Sr. was nothing short of a visionary. History certainly has proven that to be a fact. France knew that he was on to something with the success of his Daytona Beach races during the early to mid-1940s. But his glimpse of a glorious future was made possible only by two unrelated pieces of history that unexpectedly came together.

The first piece fell into place when oilman Henry Flagler began buying up the existing railroad systems in northern Florida. By 1889 he had extended the service from Jacksonville to Daytona. At that time, Daytona's roads were terribly underdeveloped, so the railway system allowed more people access to the area's twenty-six miles of flat beach.

Eventually known as the Florida East Coast Railway, its trains gave access to the second piece of France's grand design: modified moonshine cars. France had been exposed to these cars in the late 1930s when traveling to North Carolina for oval track races.

"He asked around for people to bring their liquor cars down to Daytona," Bryant McMurray says. "People like Roy Hall hauled whiskey on Saturday nights and could race a car on Sunday. Everything kind of came together. It was a show made for liquor cars."[1]

By 1945 France realized that he had a big business in the making, and those cars held the keys to his impending success. The proposition was equally attractive to the moonshiners. They could run moonshine on Saturday night and run in the stock car race on Sunday. But there was an inherent tradeoff that France was forced to make in the process. His events greatly benefited from the presence of the faster cars, but he also had to deal with the unseemly financial connection to a shady environment and the likes of car owner Raymond Parks.

"Parks wasn't an officer with NASCAR, but he loaned money weekly to finance the purse," McMurray explains. "Sometimes France would put on a show in Spartanburg, for example, with three cars that would show up. He still had to pay the purse, and there might be a hundred people in the stands. He had to do that for credibility. The money that Parks loaned him came from liquor sales and other things like gambling and prostitution. The money that came from illegal things was loaned to NASCAR, but the money had to be paid back. Raymond didn't let them slide. He did not become an investor. He became a loan officer."[2]

In December 1947 France famously met with several racers and promoters at the Ebony Bar at the Streamline Hotel in Daytona Beach. By February of the next year, the National Association for Stock Car Auto Racing was officially born. On June 19, 1949, NASCAR ran its first Strictly Stock race at Charlotte Fairgrounds Speedway. In October Red Byron (who drove for Parks) became the series' first champion. That eight-race season also featured a thirty-five-year-old rookie driver, Lee Petty, who won a fall race in Carnegie, Pennsylvania.

In 1950 France renamed the Strictly Stock Series the "Grand National Series." By then, it was already just that—a national series that covered most regions of the United States. This was especially important for the Southern fans, who had no professional sports of their own. In fact, the South wouldn't get any other taste of that world until 1966, when Major League Baseball's Milwaukee Braves moved to Atlanta, and the Atlanta Falcons made its NFL debut that same year.

Taking a Knee

Despite that national appeal, NASCAR was still very much a Southern sport, largely due to the fan base, but partly due to its unique beginnings and its veiled ties to the moonshine business. Perhaps even more hush-hush was the sport's inherent relationship to the faith community. Southerners generally were quiet about their religious beliefs, and public expressions remained rare during the NASCAR earliest days.

But in an ironic twist, it wasn't a Southerner who carried out the first recorded display of faith, but rather a driver from Oregon, Hershel McGriff. In May 1950 McGriff won the first Carrera Panamericana, a six-day Mexican road race that stretched 2,096 miles. Bill France attended that race, introduced himself to McGriff, and invited him to run at the Southern 500 later that year in Darlington, South Carolina.

"I drove from Portland down there and took the same car I won the road race with," McGriff recalls. "I finished ninth and drove it back home."[3]

There was a great deal of significance at the inaugural Southern 500. Not only was it NASCAR's first five-hundred-mile race, but also it was NASCAR's first race on a paved superspeedway. But something else happened for the first time that received much less attention. Just before the race was about to start, Hershel McGriff knelt down by his Oldsmobile 88, bowed his head, and said a brief prayer.

Up to that moment in NASCAR's brief history no one had made a public expression of faith at a race. There was a traditional singing of the national anthem, but no pre-race prayer or chapel service of any kind. McGriff's open display came naturally to the outsider. His father was a Church of God preacher and church planter.

"I was thankful for what I was able to do," McGriff says. "I just asked for the Lord to watch over me and to help me be fair about how I was going to drive. It was nothing complicated."[4]

McGriff's practice was short-lived, however, as he eventually found himself nearly missing the start of the race because of it.

"All of the sudden, they'd say 'Go!' and I wasn't even in the car yet," he explains. "So after that, if I had anything to say, I did it when I was already in the car."[5]

As a devout, nondrinking, nonsmoking Christian, McGriff found himself in the odd, but not necessarily unusual position, of driving for a moonshiner. Frank Christian was based in Dahlonega, Georgia, and McGriff operated out of his shop while racing the entire 1954 season. During the week moonshine haulers (usually young kids, as McGriff recalls) would drop by with a trunk full of the illegal product on their way to Atlanta.[6]

Other than the occasional appearance at Daytona and Talladega during the 1970s, McGriff didn't pursue a national racing career beyond 1954, instead opting to stay closer to home and run in the regional series and occasional Cup races at Riverside and Sonoma—something that he continued to do as recently as 2012, at the age of eighty-four. McGriff's most notable run happened in 1974, when he raced four times for Richard Petty that season. Although his stint in the Grand National Series was sporadic, it did leave a lasting impression.

Ned Jarrett made his NASCAR debut at the Southern 500 three years after McGriff's first appearance at the same track. Jarrett did not race against McGriff often, and their careers overlapped only by twenty-nine races over two seasons. Yet when McGriff's name is brought up, there's one thing that always come to Jarrett's mind.

"I do remember him kneeling beside his car and praying a few times," he says. "I certainly would see that. That was impressive to me. It was definitely unusual at the time. I don't think he cared [what people thought], but I don't know that anyone faulted him for doing that or felt any differently about him. I'd like to think that many of the drivers had respect for him for doing it."[7]

Gentleman Ned

Perhaps no driver had the respect of the early NASCAR community more so than Ned Jarrett, or "Gentleman Ned," as he would later become known. Jarrett had a quiet faith that was always understood, but never overstated.

Like McGriff, he grew up in a dedicated Christian home. During the week Jarrett worked on the family farm and at his dad's sawmill in Newton, North Carolina. On Sundays he went with his parents and siblings to a small nearby Lutheran Church. Jarrett was nine years old when his father started to occasionally let him drive there.

But Jarrett didn't catch the racing bug until 1951, when the Hickory Motor Speedway opened for business. The famed short track was originally run on dirt and provided an opportunity for drivers such as Junior Johnson and Ralph Earnhardt to develop their skills.

"It was a big thing for the community because there were very few forms of entertainment," Jarrett says. "You had a couple movie theaters in town and high school sports, and that was about it. Having a racetrack, that was a big thing. You'd go down to the country store on a rainy day when you couldn't work on the farm, and these farmers and saw millers would be sitting around talking: 'Boy, wait 'til they get that thing built. I'll go up there and show 'em how to drive.' Secretly I thought, 'Wow, I want to do that.'"[8]

Ironically, Jarrett's father didn't want him to race, partly because of the sport's deep connection with the moonshine business. "He couldn't see where my participation with the moonshiners could add to the image that he had worked so hard to build," Jarrett says.[9]

Jarrett drove in his first race in 1952, and his father clearly did not approve. He told Ned that he could work on cars, but not drive them. That same year, Ned filled in for his sick brother-in-law and finished second. Jarrett continued to race under assumed names, but his first victory was too difficult to keep from his father's knowledge. At that point, the elder Jarrett knew that there was little he could do to keep his son from racing.

Newton wasn't particularly known as a hub for the moonshine business. Wilkes County, roughly a forty-mile drive to the north, was much more notorious for its involvement. So when Jarrett made his national debut in 1953, he was introduced to a whole new world full of shady characters, a world fueled by illegal commerce.

"Once I got into racing, I knew of people who were involved," Jarrett says. "In fact, it seemed like back in those days a big percentage of the drivers were involved in moonshine, one way or another. There were a lot of good people who were involved in moonshine. They worked hard at it. They just had a different way of making a living. For some of them, it was the only way they knew."[10]

According to Jarrett, the landscape wasn't overly populated with believers, but he and the handful of others who dotted the landscape were always welcomed figures within NASCAR community.

"I never felt any animosity as a result of being a Christian," Jarrett says. "I never tried to hide the fact that I was a Christian, but I also didn't try to push it on anyone else. Whatever beliefs they had, that was their business, and the beliefs that I had were my business. I didn't try to get up and preach, because I wasn't capable of doing that. I don't think God put me on the earth for that, or he would have led me in a different direction."[11]

Heading into the 1964 season, Jarrett had already won his first Grand National Series championship (1961) and twenty-two career races. He quickly added to that win total by taking the season-opening checkered flag at Concord Speedway. But his celebratory mood took a quick turn just four races later, on January 19, when Joe Weatherly died from head injuries sustained during the contest at Riverside International Raceway. No one could have known the ominous tone that the tragedy would set for the rest of the year.

On May 23 Jarrett was sitting by the pool at the motel where he was staying in Charlotte awaiting the next day's World 600. He was joined by one of the sport's true superstars, Glenn "Fireball" Roberts, who had already amassed thirty-three career wins, including the 1962 Daytona 500 and a pair of Southern 500 victories in 1958 and 1963.

"Fireball and I had become pretty good friends," Jarrett remembers. "[That night] he was talking about how he was going to quit driving at the end of the year. He had an opportunity to become a spokesperson for a large company [Falstaff Brewing Company]. I don't recall in that conversation with Fireball if [previous deaths in the sport] had anything to do with his thinking about retiring or not, but I guess deep down, it would have to have some bearing, especially when you have children. Fireball had one child. You want to be there for them. Seeing all these things happen, it deep down has to have some bearing on [that decision]."[12]

The next day, on the seventh lap, Jarrett's conversation with Roberts took on profound significance. Jarrett collided with Junior Johnson, and Roberts scrambled to avoid the crash. He was able to divert from his fellow drivers, but he slammed backward into the inside retaining wall. Roberts's car flipped and burst into flames.

Roberts screamed for Jarrett's help. Jarrett ran from his car and pulled his friend out of the blazing wreckage. Although Roberts sustained burns over 80 percent of his body, he began a slow recovery process that gave doctors hope that he would survive. But on June 30 Roberts was stricken with pneumonia and sepsis, and he went into a coma the next day. By July 2, 1964, Fireball Roberts was gone.

"Certainly, I did ask myself some hard questions," Jarrett admits. "Is this what God wants me to do?"[13]

The soul-searching didn't stop there. Jimmy Pardue died on September 22 that same year after a blown tire during a tire test at

Charlotte Motor Speedway resulted in a violent, fatal crash. NASCAR lost another driver on January 5, 1965, during a tire test at Daytona. Billy Wade was killed when his car spun out on the backstretch and then hit the outside wall head-on.

But Jarrett remained secure in his decision to continue racing. It wasn't based on finances or a personal desire to be the best, but rather on a much deeper conviction of faith.

"Things were happening along that time that led me to believe that God had put me in that position," Jarrett says. "He led me to become a race car driver. When I was growing up in school, I did not have any thoughts about [being a driver]. No one in my family had ever been involved in the sport. But I felt strongly as time went by that [God] was using me."[14]

Although the string of tragic deaths from the past twelve months certainly troubled Jarrett, he never actually considered retiring until professional circumstances arose later the next season. As far as he was concerned, there was still plenty left in his proverbial tank, and there were substantial goals not yet attained.

One of the races that Jarrett wanted to win the most was the Southern 500. At that time the Daytona 500 had not yet risen to its status as "The Great American Race," and it was the Darlington event that in fact was considered NASCAR's premier event.

"It was *the* race that you wanted to win," Jarrett says.[15]

Back then, the event was run on Labor Day, so when Darlington Raceway president Bob Colvin asked Jarrett to speak to the youth group at his Methodist church the Sunday night before, he gladly accepted the offer. At the end of his talk he asked the group to pray for him. After they assured him that they would, he added another request: "It's okay with me if you go ahead and ask God to let me win."[16]

The next day, September 6, 1965, Jarrett was in his pit getting ready for the race and going over what little strategy they had back in that simpler era. As he was talking things through with his crew, a man walked up to him and introduced himself as a minister from nearby Orangeburg, South Carolina.

"I have a strong feeling today that you're going to win this race," he boldly proclaimed.

"Really?" Jarrett responded. "Well, I appreciate that."

"I had this same feeling in 1963," the man continued. "I was here, and I told Fireball Roberts the same thing that I'm telling you, and he won the race. I just wanted you to know that I feel that same way today."

Jarrett was immediately reminded of his encounter with the Methodist youth group the night before, and now he had a preacher adding to the intrigue.

"Man, they had to pull me back down out of the clouds to get me in the race car," he says. "This was wonderful."[17]

The 1965 Southern 500 turned out to be a wild affair and is still considered one of the most memorable races in NASCAR history. Of the forty-four drivers who started the race, only fifteen managed to finish. Cale Yarborough survived a nasty wreck with Sam McQuagg that caused the future Hall of Famer to fly over the guardrail and roll his car six times before coming to a stop in the parking lot.

With forty-four laps to go, race leaders Fred Lorenzon and Darel Dieringer experienced engine problems, and both were knocked out of contention. This allowed Jarrett to take a wide lead, but his good fortune wasn't without his own set of problems.

"God definitely intervened," Jarrett says. "My car was overheating the last hundred miles of that race, which was a common thing back in those days at that racetrack. There was no reason for that engine to live. Every time I mashed the accelerator, the temperature gauge would only go to 240 degrees and it was pegged to go over 240. Then something, with about fifty miles to go, told me to, instead of backing off to go into the corner, just turn the (engine) switch off and let the gasoline roll in and it would have a cooling effect. I have no idea where that came from. Nobody had ever told me that. But I started doing that and that engine cooled down 30 to 40 degrees every time. I'd flip the switch back on and it would heat back up until we got to the next turn, but it would always cool down. That helped me to finish that race. I'll never believe anything else except that God had his hand on that situation that day and put those thoughts in my mind what to do."[18]

Jarrett won the race by fourteen laps (just over nineteen miles), which is the record for farthest margin of victory in a NASCAR race. Jarrett has no problem remembering Buck Baker, the driver who finished a distant second. As for the preacher who spoke to him before the race, Jarrett never saw him again and to this day can't remember his name.

The usual celebratory mood in Victory Lane was muted, however, by an accident that had taken place way back on the second lap some four hours earlier. A twenty-eight-year-old rookie driver, Buren Skeen, spun out and was hit on his driver's side. Although his car was bent nearly in half, Skeen initially survived the crash, but he died of complications seven days later.

As NASCAR trudged ahead with its final ten races, Jarrett continued his phenomenal run with seven top-five finishes, including a victory in the season-ending event at the Dog Track Speedway in Moyock, North Carolina. His efforts were more than enough to capture a second Grand National Series championship.

Jarrett was poised to compete for a third title in 1966 when Ford announced it was withdrawing its cars from NASCAR competition. After racing in eight of the first nine races, the seasoned veteran decided it was time to retire at the age of thirty-four. Jarrett would race in thirteen of the remaining thirty-nine events, including the season-ending American 500 in Rockingham, but his desire to go out a champion was essentially fulfilled.

"I vowed to myself early on that however far up the ladder I got, I would quit while I was there and not go down the other side," he says. "People have a tendency to remember the last thing you did, and I didn't want them to remember me as a has-been."[19]

There were other reasons as well. Jarrett had been missing out on much of his three children's lives and was ready to slow down for a while. And although it wasn't among the three primary factors, Jarrett admits that the rash of racetrack deaths also made it easier for him to step out from behind the wheel. Ironically, Junior Johnson also officially retired after that final race in Rockingham. It was Johnson whose wreck with Jarrett had caused Fireball Roberts's fatal crash a year earlier at the World 600 in Charlotte.

Jarrett's impact on the sport would continue as a popular broadcaster, but his presence as a Christian driver set the tone for things to come. Even then, Richard Petty had become another subdued man of faith in the garage. There was also the quiet presence of the Wood Brothers dating back to 1950. But while Jarrett sometimes wonders if there were more people like him at the time, he does think that he knows why they weren't outward in their expressions of faith.

"In those days there were not many that had much of an education," he explains. "They were somewhat bashful about their beliefs. They didn't care to expose them. I'm sure there were more people that had a lot of faith than what we knew about, but they kept it to themselves."[20]

Shalom and Amen

It was, ironically, at the 1953 Southern 500, the same race where Jarrett debuted, when another Christian driver first hit the NASCAR scene. Marvin Panch started his racing career as a car owner in Oakland, California, but he got behind the wheel when his driver didn't show up for a race. Panch became a fixture in the series over the next several years, with seventeen Grand National Series wins, including the 1961 Daytona 500.

In 1955 one of the first truly outspoken Christians made his NASCAR debut. He was Marion Cox, a car owner from Hemingway, South Carolina.

"They called him Preacher," NASCAR Hall of Fame historian Buz McKim says. "He looked just like a bulldog. He was amazing."[21]

But Cox's religious convictions kept him from competing in most Grand National Series races because the series primarily ran on Sundays. Cox didn't believe that he should race on the Sabbath. In fact, the burly World War II veteran would later pull one of his cars from a Saturday night event that continued past midnight and into early Sunday morning due to numerous delays.

"He would strictly run the late-model class," McKim adds. "He always raced on Saturday or Friday night. He built such a great car that he could have been extremely successful on the big circuit, but he chose not to."[22]

In 1965 another NASCAR fixture stepped away from the sport due to his faith. Ray Lee Wood was the tire changer for his brothers' famed #21 car. But while working for driver Jim Clark and Team Lotus at the Indianapolis 500, Wood "felt the calling of the Lord."

"He had something else for me to do," Wood recalls.[23]

Wood vowed to finish out the NASCAR season with driver Curtis Turner, and he did so in spectacular fashion. Turner won the inaugural American 500 at Rockingham in the final race. Wood then retired to spend more time working with a Pentecostal Holiness church near his home in Buffalo Ridge, Virginia.[24]

Delano Wood followed his brother Ray Lee's footsteps eighteen years later, leaving his job as jack man to likewise engage in ministry endeavors. The remaining Wood brothers stood firm in their personal convictions as well.

"Back in the '70s, one of the main liquor companies was making whiskey decanters of all the top cars," McKim says. "The Wood brothers had an opportunity to make some big money on the deal, but they chose not to because it would go against their principles."[25]

Throughout NASCAR's early years Christians within the sport such as Jarrett, Petty, and the Wood brothers usually held their beliefs close to the vest. Outside of the occasional "God bless this race" or similarly simplistic pre-event prayers, public expressions of faith were also rare.

That all changed on February 22, 1959. Earlier that year, a young preacher, Rev. Hal Marchman, became the pastor at Central Baptist Church in Daytona. He also happened to be friends with Bill France Sr. As the inaugural Daytona 500 approached, France asked Marchman to give an invocation before the race. Eventually, Marchman would become known as the speedway's chaplain, and for forty-six years he said the prayer at all of its races throughout the season.

Marchman retired from that role in 2005, but not before adding a new wrinkle to his presentation. Instead of ending his prayers with the customary "Amen," he instead began saying "Shalom and amen" in an attempt to be more inclusive.[26]

Not only did the Baptist minister assist injured drivers and their families, but also he developed close relationships with the NASCAR community, even officiating the marriages of some couples within the community, including McKim and his wife.[27]

But perhaps most importantly, Marchman set the tone for the pre-race prayer to become a common occurrence. Ned Jarrett, for instance, recalls pre-race prayers at Charlotte in 1961 and 1962. Marchman would also travel to Talladega on occasion and give the invocation there after its opening in 1969. Today, NASCAR remains the only national professional sports organization that has sanctioned prayer before the start of all of its competitive events.

As the sport grew in popularity, NASCAR was also starting to face some problems within its organization. Even though America's tumultuous 1960s were coming to a close, stock car racing still had many challenges to overcome. On the other hand, there were glimpses of glory on the horizon—not just for

NASCAR, but also for a growing faith movement that was steadily building inside the stock car racing beltway.

NOTES

1. Bryant McMurray, interview with the author, September 17, 2012.
2. Ibid.
3. Hershel McGriff, interview with the author, September 17, 2012.
4. Ibid.
5. Ibid.
6. Ibid.
7. Ned Jarrett, interview with the author, August 21, 2012.
8. Ibid.
9. Ibid.
10. Ibid.
11. Ibid.
12. Ibid.
13. Ibid.
14. Ibid.
15. Ibid.
16. Ibid.
17. Ibid.
18. Ibid.
19. Ibid.
20. Ibid.
21. Buz McKim, interview with the author, January 31, 2012.
22. Ibid.
23. "Racing Wasn't the Only Callling for One of the Original Wood Brothers," http://woodbrothersracing.com/?p=2106 (accessed July 11, 2013).
24. Ibid.
25. Buz McKim, interview with the author, January 31, 2012.
26. Ibid.
27. Ibid.

CHAPTER 3

Church on Wheels

After twenty years of steady growth, NASCAR was poised to take the next step in its evolutionary progression, and Bill France Sr. had something big in mind. These days, it's known as Talladega Superspeedway, but from its debut in 1969 until 1989, the monstrous 2.66-mile tri-oval[1] was known as the Alabama International Motor Speedway. France broke ground on the facility on May 23, 1968, and it was ready for its Grand National debut by September 1969.

Up until the 1969 season, there were no signs of organized ministry for the quickly expanding NASCAR family, and Rev. Hal Marchman was still one of the few known spiritual leaders in the racing community. NASCAR Hall of Fame inductee Bobby Allison recalls random preachers who would show up and serve as unofficial chaplains.

"A lot of times there was some kind of mention at the driver's meeting, you know, 'Lord bless this day for us,'" Allison recalls. "Somebody from NASCAR would make a comment. [Pre-race prayer] went on from time to time. It might happen at a race and then not happen at the next race. Sometimes there would be some minister from the area of the particular racetrack. NASCAR would allow that to go on."[2] Although he had retired in 1966, Ned Jarrett remained a fixture around the sport due to his foray into the broadcasting world, and he often took on the role of spiritual figurehead in those days when NASCAR had no official ministry presence.

"I began to be asked to do invocations," Jarrett says. "It seemed like for twenty years that I was the official person to give the invocation, whether it was at a dinner or, many times, at the racetrack before the race, just whatever the occasion might be. I was flattered by that, but there again, I felt like God put me in the position to do this. I just felt strongly that this was why he wanted me to stay in the sport as long as I did and have an influence one way or another on his work."[3]

But much like NASCAR's early history, the sport was made up mostly of drivers who weren't terribly interested in wearing their Christian faith on their sleeves—or anywhere else on their sponsor-riddled fire suits, for that matter.

"A lot of the guys weren't expressive like that in the old days," Buz McKim says. "In fact, a lot of the drivers from the late '60s and early '70s were known to be philanderers, guys like Cruise Turner, Buck Baker, and people like that. That was the image of the drivers back then."[4]

That negative association was slowly changing. In fact, when R. J. Reynolds became NASCAR'S first major corporate sponsor in 1972, CEO Bill Hobbs declared to the racing community ahead of the Talladega race that the organization moving forward would be presented as a family sport.[5]

Jarrett certainly had already helped change the perception of NASCAR as a sport made up mostly of rabble-rousers, moonshiners, and uneducated rednecks. Richard Petty was also a major influence. He and rising stars such as Allison were family men who were helping to reshape public opinion.

Before the sport could truly find its way, however, it needed the help of a spiritual mentor, and up until 1970 there was no such leader guiding NASCAR's path from week to week throughout the season.

Brother Bill

When Bill Frazier, a reformed alcoholic turned minister, heard that Bill France Sr. was building a track near Talladega, he was immediately intrigued. But it wasn't until his annual trip to the Daytona 500 that the Gadsden, Alabama, resident started to see the big picture develop in his mind's eye.

At that first Talladega race in 1969 Frazier wondered if anyone was tending to the racing teams' spiritual needs. He was even more troubled by the realization that the forty-week schedule likely kept most of the participants out of Sunday church services. His concern was compounded by the fact that there were roughly five hundred people who traveled the circuit, including drivers, crew members, officials, sponsors, and their family members.[6]

Perhaps no one has gotten more of a look into Frazier's life than Racers For Christ chaplain Richard Guy. His book *With God You're Always a Winner* chronicles Frazier's story and what motivated him to pioneer a brand new kind of ministry.

"When he came back to the Lord, he came back hard," Guy explains. "He was very active in his church. He was made a deacon. He started looking for something to do. Bill had friends who raced, and he started going to short track and dirt track races out in western Alabama. At Daytona, that's where he first saw the opportunity to minister to hundreds of people. He felt called to do it."[7]

September 14, 1969, seemed like the perfect time to get started. Talladega was less than sixty miles south of Gadsden, so Frazier drove his pickup truck and made his way to the historic opening of the France family's new track there.

That first weekend, Frazier operated out of the back of his truck. He walked around the infield, handed out Christian pamphlets, and introduced himself to anyone who would listen as "God's public relations man."[8]

What Frazier didn't realize was that he had, in fact, picked perhaps the worst race possible to test the ministry waters. Earlier that month several of the top drivers had formed the Professional Drivers Association (PDA). Back in 1961 France had squashed Curtis Turner's attempt to unionize the NASCAR garage and actually banned the driver for life, although the ban was lifted after four years. But this time Petty headed the new association, along with heavy hitters such as Allison, Buddy Baker, David Pearson, and Cale Yarborough.[9]

The drivers had a variety of concerns, including safety issues on the track and increasingly unsavory conditions in the infield, where their families were exposed to unruly fans engaging in wild, nonstop parties.[10]

Ultimately, it came down to the tires. The PDA wanted a safer tire for Talladega's unprecedented speeds, but France refused to postpone the race in order to give Goodyear time to come up with an agreeable solution. When France gave the drivers an ultimatum, the members of the PDA walked out. But France, the NASCAR CEO, refused to be upstaged, and he put together a thirty-six-car field pulled from the previous day's Grand American series contest.[11] The Grand American series was a secondary NASCAR-sanctioned series that ran from 1968 to 1971.

The following week, NASCAR officials met with race promoters in Charlotte to find a solution to the complaints registered by the Grand National regulars. This action essentially killed the PDA.[12]

Bill Frazier was understandably disappointed. The chaos caused by the labor dispute essentially ended his chance to make an impact in the garage that weekend. But Frazier refused to let his vision die. He came back the next year for Talladega's spring race and even brought a gospel music quartet to attract attention to his ministry efforts. Unfortunately, torrential rains throughout much of the weekend impeded Frazier's efforts, and he once again went home discouraged.[13]

In July Frazier took some vacation time away from his job at the steel mill and made a trip to Daytona for the Firecracker 400. But he wasn't really there to see the race so much as to consult with Marchman. The established local minister advised Frazier to reach out to the track promoters and ask them if they were interested in having him provide ministry at their events. Only three of the thirty people he contacted responded. Many would have been too discouraged to continue, but Frazier determinedly, if not stubbornly, trudged ahead.[14]

Church on Wheels

Driving home from Daytona, Frazier saw a mobile chapel sitting in front of a church; the chapel could be pulled like a trailer and used for children's outreach events. He had already been contemplating a better way to preach than from the bed of his truck, and this seemed to be the perfect solution. Back in Gadsden, he sold some possessions and set aside some earnings from his job. With that money he bought a single-axle trailer and built his house of worship onto it. The little church building had six two-person pews, and a makeshift sign on the side of the building to the right of the door simply said, "The Chapel."[15]

Just like his previous two attempts, Frazier showed up in Talladega unannounced, but this time the bold preacher brought the church on wheels with him. A few days earlier, Frazier had asked the track manager for permission to park on the infield. The gentleman needed to be convinced, but ultimately it was the manager's own personal faith in God that compelled him to give Frazier a pass that would get the minister and his mobile chapel through the gate.[16]

On August 23, 1970, the morning of the Talladega 500, Frazier stood along the fence that served as a barrier between the drivers in the garage and the fans in the infield. Bryant McMurray was working as a photographer at the time and watched the situation unfold with a skeptical eye.

"Religion is an easy venue to scam with," McMurray says. "You could set up a church in the infield in [the late 1950s or early 1960s], and you could take up collections, and you could go from town to town and make a pretty good living at it. I don't know if it satisfied the religious needs of the fans or the drivers, but that's the way it was."[17]

McMurray wasn't the only curious onlooker. When drivers needed to use the restroom, they had to walk out into the infield among the race goers. That was a perfect opportunity for Frazier to engage the drivers and their crews. A few minutes before his scheduled 9:00 a.m. service, he engaged two men who had walked from the garage to the restroom. In the process, Frazier introduced himself and invited them to chapel.

"One of the men used some pretty salty language," Guy says. "But essentially he was telling Bill, 'I don't care what you do.'"[18]

But to Frazier's surprise, the two men showed up at the chapel right about time for the service to start. The man who had talked to him turned out to be Richard Petty's brother, Maurice Petty, chief engine builder for Petty Enterprises. Like many others who saw Frazier's chapel that day, Petty described the little building as "an outhouse on wheels."[19]

As Frazier was about to begin preaching, driver Neil "Soapy" Castles and two of his crew members showed up along with two kids who followed them in out of curiosity. With seven people in the congregation, Frazier held what is believed to be the first pre-race chapel service in NASCAR history.[20]

"The first person who came to the chapel was Maurice Petty," Frazier said in an interview the following year. "[His car, driven by Pete Hamilton,] won the race that day. The last man who walked in was Soapy Castle, and Soapy blew his engine and was the first man out. It just kind of ironically worked out that way."[21]

That interview wasn't the first attention that Frazier received from the press. At that first appearance in Talladega, *Sports Illustrated* writer Robert Creamer noticed the little chapel and stopped by to ask Frazier some questions. The result of that conversation showed up in the magazine a week later.

"You see Goodyear, Prestone, Grey-Rock and just about everything else you can think of at these races," Frazier told Creamer. "I figured it was time the Lord got a little representation. I'm going to promote God just like the other guys promote STP. . . . [The drivers are] so close to death they don't want to think about it. But wives like the idea, and occasionally a driver will ask me to pray for an engine."[22]

Petty Country

Richard Petty didn't attend that first service with his brother, but he did take note of what was taking place. Eventually he would become a key piece in ensuring that ministry to the NASCAR community was part of the weekly routine.

"We went to Talladega one day and here Bill had him a little rig-a-ma-roo out there in the infield and he decided he was going to save everybody," Petty says. "Right out of the blue, here he comes. He and my brother hit it off real good."[23]

Along with the Pettys, one of Frazier's first major supporters was Bobby Allison. Although a staunch Catholic, he was instantly impressed with Frazier and his desire to hold a nondenominational service at the track throughout the season.

"[Frazier] showed up with that [chapel], and he was very friendly," Allison recalls. "I talked to him along the way, and he said hello and that he was a big fan of mine from there in Alabama, and he was glad I was doing good, and he was going to have a little church service after the driver's meeting. He really wanted me to come to his nondenominational service. He knew I was Catholic, but he still wanted me to stop by if I would. So I eventually did, and I was really impressed with him and really pleased with his effort."[24]

Allison went to NASCAR competition director Bill Gazaway and told him about Frazier. Initially, Gazaway was agreeable to Allison's request, but his brother, Joe Gazaway, the technical inspector, never seemed to be accepting of it.

"Over time, Bill started to feel like we were too professional to have someone around there wanting to pray," Allison says. "He had that attitude."[25]

But initially, the driver support overrode any potential problems. It didn't take long for attendance to outgrow the chapel's meager twelve-person capacity. Just a few weeks into it, Allison helped set chairs out in front of the building to accommodate the growing crowd.

"I didn't always go to the services with Bill because I went to mass or I'd been to mass," he says. "Bill knew that I supported him, and we were friends. I did not go to a lot of his services, but I did go to a few. I continued to really have a high regard for him, even to the point where I would take him in my Lear plane and take him to some events so he didn't have to drive his car."[26]

After his first experience at Talladega, Frazier next showed up two weeks later at the Southern 500 in Darlington. When he arrived at the track to prepare for Sunday service, he discovered that his chapel had been moved and trashed by race fans who had used the building as a party house the night before.[27]

But Frazier's discouragement over this minor setback was alleviated when he received a letter from Maurice Petty inviting him to visit Petty Enterprises. Frazier was especially shocked to see that Petty had also inserted a donation of five hundred dollars.[28]

"Bill went to the Petty's garage and met Richard," Guy says. "Richard saw it immediately. He had a young family, and he felt like [Bill's ministry] was a good thing. It was pretty rough at the track. No women were allowed in the pits. Families weren't allowed in the pits. It was rough out there because they were out there with all of those drunk fans. They were happy to see something that would help change things."[29]

Petty also appreciated Frazier's plainspoken approach. His brother Maurice and sister-and-law Patty would later say that Frazier was the one preacher who could always explain spiritual matters to them in "plain terms."[30]

The Pettys began helping Frazier get credentials to the races. At the same time, NASCAR employee Eva Williams, also a devout Christian, began granting Frazier garage passes despite her bosses' instructions not to do so.[31]

In a strange if not providential twist, Frazier's presence brought together two of NASCAR fiercest rivals. There was no love lost between the Pettys and Bobby Allison. The two teams notoriously battled for race wins and Cup championships throughout the 1970s, including an infamous final-lap collision at the North Wilkesboro Speedway on October 1, 1972. After Petty won the race, both sides were quick to say their piece, and a drunken fan tainted the Victory Lane celebration when he hopped the fence and attempted to attack the winning driver. He failed thanks to a helmet wielded by Maurice Petty.[32]

So it must have seemed strange to race fans when Petty and Allison publicly joined forces to support Frazier. For instance, Petty sold square-inch pieces of his Level Cross property for two dollars each. Fans would get a certificate of their purchase of this deeded land referred to as "Petty Country." All of the money went to Chapel Inc., an organization that supported Frazier's ministry and included Petty and Allison as board members. Allison himself bought a piece of Petty Country and promoted the fundraiser in *Stock Car Magazine*.[33]

"The Allisons and the Pettys were not friends," Guy says. "But for the ministry, they came together."[34]

Frazier's mobile chapel survived only six races during his initial part-time season on the circuit. It was dislodged from his trailer on the way to the American 500 at Rockingham and abandoned along I-85. But by then, the little church on wheels had served its purpose.[35]

"The chapel was really just a gimmick to get people's attention in the infield," Guy says.[36]

Frazier next used a tent that held about twenty people. By May 1971, during his first full-time season as chaplain, the tent was overflowing with about twenty-five people attending chapel service. By June of that year, his meetings had grown to about sixty-five people.[37]

Head NASCAR scorer Morris Metcalfe took note of Frazier's dilemma and suggested that he hold his service in the scorers' stands. In August 1971 at Talladega more than two hundred people gathered in that setting to hear the Sunday morning sermon.[38]

That same year, some NASCAR officials began asking Frazier to close drivers' meetings with prayer. A. J. Foyt took note of Frazier's efforts but never actually attended one of his services. Known for his exploits as an open-wheel driver, Foyt felt like an outsider and, other than the drivers' meetings, rarely hung out with the other men in large group settings. But on April 4, 1971, the morning of the Atlanta 500, Foyt randomly walked up to Frazier and handed him a donation of twenty dollars. Foyt went on to win that race for car owner Glen Wood. It was his fifth of seven career Cup victories.[39]

The year 1972 turned out to be a pivotal one for both NASCAR and Bill Frazier. On January 10 Bill France Sr. handed over his responsibilities to Bill France Jr., whose first major act of business was announcing the arrival of R. J. Reynolds Company as NASCAR's headlining sponsor and the series name change to "Winston Cup."

For Frazier, the ministry was booming. He took in fourteen thousand dollars in donations that year and was generally free of the week-to-week financial worries.[40]

On May 7, at Talladega, track general manager Don Namon arranged for Frazier's chapel service to be piped through the grandstand's PA system. The following year on September 30, at Martinsville, track owner Clay Earles allowed Frazier to hold his meeting on the straightaway. The scene was filmed and used in the Junior Johnson biopic *The Last American Hero*.[41]

Frazier also pioneered another pre-race tradition. Allison recalls that Frazier was the first minister to routinely run up and down pit road to pray with drivers just before the start of the race.[42]

One of Frazier's more popular concepts was The Racer's Prayer, which was routinely seen on car decals and fire suit patches. The logo featured a checkered flag and a Christian flag. Below the flags was the slogan "With God, You're Always a Winner," followed by these simple, but effective words:

> *Lord, I pray as I race today,*
> *Keep me safe along the way,*
> *Not only me but others too*
> *As they perform the jobs they do.*
>
> *I know, God, that in a race*
> *I, the driver, must set the pace.*
> *But in this race of life, I pray,*
> *Help me, Lord, along the way.*
>
> *Although I know I am a sinner,*
> *Help me to believe, that with*
> *GOD you're always a winner.*[43]

Running Interference

Over time, Frazier's support continued to grow. Allison points to other drivers, such as James Hylton, Elmo Langley, John Sears,

Frank Warren, Cecil Gordon, and Richard Childress, who were among those to attend chapel services and occasionally slip Frazier some expense money or take care of various obligations.

"They weren't conspicuous, but they weren't totally hidden," Allison says. "You'd see it if you were paying attention."[44]

Even with many drivers on his side, Frazier still had to deal with the fact that some NASCAR officials and track owners didn't want him around. Bill Gazaway was one of Frazier's early opponents.

"Bill Frazier would ask Gazaway about tech inspection times so he could schedule chapel around those times," Guy says. "Then Gazaway would change his time at the last minute to create a conflict with the chapel service."[45]

And while many of the drivers initially assumed that it was simply Gazaway's personal aversion to religious expression at the track that dictated his actions, Frazier would come to learn that the interference was actually coming as a direct order from the top. Bill France Sr. felt that Frazier's presence could potentially undercut his control of the garage.[46]

Frazier also found adverse conditions at a few of the tracks. Throughout the 1960s and 1970s Riverside Speedway was a popular West Coast stop on the NASCAR circuit. At the 1971 Grand National race there, Frazier made the rare mistake of failing to secure permission from the track promoter to hold a chapel service on Sunday. Los Angeles Rams football player Les Richter owned the speedway and relied on his former teammate Roy Hord to manage the track. Just thirty minutes before Frazier was set to preach to congregants in the scorers' stands, track officials announced that the service had been cancelled. As Frazier stood in disbelief, Goodyear Tire race representative Chuck Blanchard offered his company's garage as a replacement host for morning chapel.[47]

"God always intervened every time somebody tried to stop it," Guy says.[48]

Promoter or Preacher?

Throughout the 1970s NASCAR continued to go through many changes. Car manufacturers fluctuated in their levels of support. Old sponsors left, and new sponsors came onto the scene. And legendary drivers found themselves facing greater challenges from upstart operations that were once deemed too underfunded to compete with the big boys.

Bill Frazier was also experiencing significant changes in his life. The ministry clearly was making a difference within the garage, but his time away from his wife and children was taking its toll. In 1973 Richard Petty found a way to help rectify the situation. He gave Frazier a house trailer and helped him place it in a mobile-home park not far from the Petty complex.[49]

Since he was around more often, Frazier offered to do odd jobs to help out around the shop. Petty took notice and decided to give Frazier some work handling his promotional affairs. It didn't take long for the driver to realize that his preacher friend had a knack for coming up with good ideas and putting them into action. Frazier too saw the potential for financial freedom, and at the start of the 1974 season he approached the Pettys with the idea for what would become known as Success Promotions.[50]

Frazier's company, true to its moniker, was a roaring success. He was one of the first to create die-cast models of race cars. Frazier also signed licensing deals with all of the major drivers and essentially created a loophole that took the power right out of NASCAR and the individual track promoters' hands.[51]

Frazier had suddenly become two different people to the drivers. On one hand, he was the trusted chaplain who would talk to them individually about their personal issues and collectively share inspirational messages each week. But on the other hand, he was also a savvy businessman who had found some creative ways to make them money.

This troubled Bryant McMurray, who by then had befriended Frazier.

"He wasn't a con man, but he was a Jim Bakker-type guy," McMurray says. "When he linked up with the Pettys, we asked ourselves, 'Does Richard really know what this guy is up to?' Once he started the souvenir business, he was pure money then. There was no religion about it. So everybody knew. He was in for the money."[52]

Although 1975 was a windfall year for Frazier's business ventures, it was a difficult year for his ministry. On May 4 Richard Petty's crew member and brother-in-law, Randy Owens, died at Talladega when a water tank exploded during the Winston 500. Two days later, Frazier preached at his funeral in Randleman.[53]

Then, on August 18, Tiny Lund was killed on the seventh lap of the Talladega 500 when Terry Link rammed into his driver's side after a multiple-car incident.[54]

Frazier was shaken by the tragedies and began to question his calling. His immediate response was to spend more time on his business. In order to maintain the ministry program that he had started five years earlier, Frazier asked a minister, Jim Adams, to oversee Sunday chapel services. He also started bringing guest speakers such as New York Yankees second baseman Bobby Richardson and North Carolina University four-sport athlete Albert Long.[55]

Albert Long spoke at the World 600 in Charlotte and recalls sharing a twelve-minute message with the NASCAR teams and officials, as well as the more than one hundred thousand fans, who provided a captive audience.

"Not many of the drivers showed up because of a last-minute change," Long says. "But Richard Petty and Cale Yarborough were there, and they came in first and second. I was overjoyed to have been a small part of what Bill Frazier started."[56]

On October 12, at the Capital City 500 in Richmond, Bill France Jr. pulled Frazier from a luxury box and asked him this pointed question: "Are you Bill Frazier the promoter, or Brother Bill the preacher?" Frazier told France that he was still both. The response wasn't satisfactory for either gentleman, but both proceeded to let it go for the time being.[57]

Deep down, however, Frazier knew he couldn't continue this way for much longer. His conflicted reality was further driven home when David Pearson, one of his longtime supporters, confronted him about what he perceived as Frazier falling away from the Lord.[58]

Before the start of the 1976 season, Frazier officially resigned as NASCAR's chaplain. His decision upset Maurice Petty perhaps more than most within the racing community, but it also greatly bothered some of the drivers' wives, such as Lynda Petty, Stevie Waltrip, and Judy Allison. They were concerned that their husbands would suffer the most from his absence.[59]

For the next two seasons NASCAR no longer enjoyed the luxury of having a singular moral voice to guide the way. It was clear to those who cared the most about the sport's spiritual well-being that eventually something would have to change.

NOTES

1. A tri-oval racetrack combines elements of the triangle and the oval shapes. While most racetracks have four turns, the tri-oval has an extra, fifth turn near the start-finish line.
2. Bobby Allison, interview with the author, February 14, 2012.
3. Ned Jarrett, interview with the author, August 21, 2012.
4. Buz McKim, interview with the author, January 31, 2012.
5. Richard Guy, *With God You're Always a Winner* (Maitland, FL: Xulon Press, 2012), 63.
6. Ibid., 21.
7. Richard Guy, interview with the author, December 19, 2012.
8. Guy, *With God You're Always a Winner*, 27.
9. Mike Harris, "Driver Boycott Killed NASCAR Union," Associated Press, February 7, 2007.
10. Guy, *With God You're Always a Winner*, 24.
11. Harris, "Driver Boycott Killed NASCAR Union."

12. Ibid.
13. Guy, *With God You're Always a Winner*, 28.
14. Ibid., 29.
15. Ibid., 31–32.
16. Richard Guy, interview with the author, December 19, 2012.
17. Bryant McMurray, interview with the author, September 17, 2012.
18. Richard Guy, interview with the author, December 19, 2012.
19. Ibid.
20. Guy, *With God You're Always a Winner*, 36–37.
21. "Evangelist Preaches to Car Races," *Florence Times — Tri-Cities Daily*, November 25, 1972.
22. Robert Creamer, "Prayer Wheels," *Sports Illustrated*, August 31, 1970.
23. Daniel S. Pierce, *Real NASCAR: White Lightning, Red Clay, and Big Bill France* (Chapel Hill: University of North Carolina Press, 2010), 285.
24. Bobby Allison, interview with the author, February 14, 2012.
25. Ibid.
26. Ibid.
27. Guy, *With God You're Always a Winner*, 39.
28. Ibid., 42.
29. Richard Guy, interview with the author, December 19, 2012.
30. Ibid.
31. Guy, *With God You're Always a Winner*, 44.
32. Ben White, "Petty, Allison Rivalry Was Tops," *The Dispatch*, September 1, 1998.
33. Guy, *With God You're Always a Winner*, 73.
34. Richard Guy, interview with the author, December 19, 2012.
35. Pierce, *Real NASCAR*, 284.
36. Richard Guy, interview with the author, December 19, 2012.
37. Guy, *With God You're Always a Winner*, 57.
38. Ibid., 50.
39. Ibid., 78.
40. Pierce, *Real NASCAR*, 285.
41. Guy, *With God You're Always a Winner*, 62–63.
42. Bobby Allison, interview with the author, February 14, 2012.
43. Guy, *With God You're Always a Winner*, 46.
44. Bobby Allison, interview with the author, February 14, 2012.
45. Richard Guy, interview with the author, December 19, 2012.
46. Ibid.
47. Guy, *With God You're Always a Winner*, 53.
48. Richard Guy, interview with the author, December 19, 2012.
49. Guy, *With God You're Always a Winner*, 65–66.
50. Ibid., 83.

51. Ibid., 86–87.
52. Bryant McMurray, interview with the author, September 17, 2012.
53. Associated Press, "Petty's Brother In Law Is Killed in Pits," *Sarasota Herald-Tribune*, May 6, 1975.
54. Jim Furlong, "Tiny Lund Killed at Talladega in Five-Car Early Race Crash," *The Tuscaloosa News*, August 18, 1975.
55. Guy, *With God You're Always a Winner*, 96–97.
56. Albert Long, interview with the author, April 7, 2013.
57. Guy, *With God You're Always a Winner*, 98.
58. Ibid., 99.
59. Ibid., 100–101.

CHAPTER 4

Motorsports Missionaries

Sometimes being in the moment doesn't allow for a clear view of the big picture. When Brother Bill Frazier stepped away from his duties as NASCAR chaplain in 1976, it's not likely that the racing community had the right perspective to understand exactly what he had done. In fact, Frazier had pioneered one of the first major sports chaplaincy programs and had set NASCAR on a path toward greater spiritual growth.

Even after Frazier resigned, he still did his best to make sure that ministry was happening at the track. Local pastors and other constant figures like Rev. Hal Marchman continued to fill the gaps.

Although many of the core racing teams would have preferred something more consistent, the sport's biggest stars were too busy pushing NASCAR toward the front of the nation's collective consciousness. It all started on February 15, 1976, at the Daytona 500, where David Pearson and Richard Petty famously battled it out on the last lap. After the two wrecked near the finish line, Petty and his iconic #43 Dodge stalled out in the grass just a few yards from the checkered flag, while Pearson managed to get back on the track and force his #21 Mercury across the line for the win.

An estimated 18.3 million viewers watched the ending of the race live on ABC's *Wide World of Sports*, providing what has often been considered one of the sport's watershed television broadcasts.

By the end of the 1976 season, NASCAR had officially become the top motorsports draw worldwide, with more than 1.4 million spectators attending thirty events.[1]

Motorsports Missionaries

NASCAR races were also attracting increasingly large crowds of campers on the infields and outside of the tracks to the tune of hundreds of thousands. This fact did not go unnoticed by Frank Stark. The pastor from Missouri showed up at the 1976 Daytona 500 with his wife and 125,000 race fans. As he looked around the campground where he was staying, Stark was struck by a thought similar to the one that Bill Frazier had seven years earlier at the same event.

"Frank saw all those people and thought that somebody should be doing something," former Raceway Ministries CEO Roger Marsh says. "So he told his wife, Betty, to go stand at an intersection by a couple of pedestrian walkways. He would send fans over to her until eventually he had gathered twenty or thirty fans together for an impromptu chapel service."[2]

Stark didn't stop there. He traveled to Atlanta and Talladega and organized informal ministry outreaches at those racetracks. He eventually found support from Talladega promoter Don Namon and Atlanta CEO Ed Clark. Both were supportive of Starks's fledgling ministry and allowed him to operate freely within the race fan community.

That same year, Ed Quattlebaum attended a missions conference in South Carolina at which one of the speakers suggested that Darlington Speedway needed outreach ministry. Quattlebaum was the director of missions for Welsh Neck Baptist Association, and the statement immediately resonated within his heart and mind.

"It hit me like a ton of bricks right between the eyes," he recalls in an interview with *The Courier*, a South Carolina Baptist publication.

"We felt so strongly that God wanted us to do this ministry, we launched out on faith, believing that He would supply what we needed, and He did."[3]

For the following NASCAR race, Quattlebaum borrowed a tent from a funeral home and set it up across the street from the speedway. He served water to the fans as they walked by and handed them gospel tracts.[4] The handouts contained the following message: "The greatest race of all cannot be run in a Ford, Chevrolet or Plymouth, but it can be won by giving your life to Jesus Christ."[5]

A couple of years later in Daytona, Stark and Quattlebaum connected with Marchman, who had been serving as chaplain for the competitors there as an outreach of Central Baptist Church since 1959. Marchman was also providing childcare for the drivers and their teams. The three men met in Marchman's office and "began talking and dreaming." Their collective efforts eventually took the concept of fan-based ministry to other locations such as Rockingham, North Wilkesboro, Myrtle Beach, Martinsville, and Dover.[6]

In 1997 Marsh joined what by then had become known as the National Fellowship of Raceway Ministries (NFRM) when he helped launch the upstart Texas Alliance Raceway Ministries. Eventually he was elected to serve as the third president of the national group in 2001, following Jim McBride (director of Dover Raceway Ministries) and John Fox (director of Raceway Ministries Martinsville), and then he became the NFRM's first executive director in 2004.

Marsh says that a big part of NFRM's early success during the late '70s and early '80s was due to support from the racing community.

"When we had ministry going on at Darlington, Atlanta, and Talladega, Darrell Waltrip and Lake Speed would volunteer to go out to the ministry site and spend time hanging out with the fans and sharing their testimonies," he says. "That was huge. If you had a NASCAR driver out, then that was going to draw fans and it did. That legitimized everything. It built some tremendous bridges."[7]

Another Brother Bill

Although superstars such as Richard Petty and Bobby Allison were instrumental in bringing NASCAR's first official chaplain into the sport, Bill Frazier's eventual successor was introduced to the racing community by a less likely source and through a completely different set of circumstances.

In 1977 a minister, Bill Baird, was preaching at a crusade in Timmonsville, South Carolina. It just so happened that Cale Yarborough's mother, Annie, was at one of those services. Afterward, she struck up a conversation with the magnanimous evangelist and told him that her son and the other drivers had need of a new chaplain.

"Although I had never seen a stock-car race, I liked the idea," Baird once told Tom Archdeacon of *The Miami News*. "Eventually, I talked to Cale and Richard Petty and Benny Parsons, and they all told me they wanted to have their own church at the tracks. There wasn't a lot of money involved, but they needed someone to put in time and dedication, and I decided to take the challenge."[8]

Much like Frazier, Baird had experienced a radical spiritual transformation. He grew up in a Quaker family in Asheboro, North Carolina, where he attended high school and then played football at Guilford College. After graduating in 1969, Baird got a tryout with the Minnesota Vikings, but eventually he was cut during training camp.

"After I got cut by the Vikings, I felt like my life was going nowhere," Baird told Archdeacon. "I was a real rebel. I looked for excuses to get into confrontations. I was just a violent-type person who didn't respect too much.... I ran the full gamut of vices and still ended up with zero. One thing I will tell you, I hated preachers."[9]

In another strange twist, the man who led Baird back to God was the same man who had made a significant impact on Frazier's life. He was Bob Harrington, and he was commonly known as "The Chaplain of Bourbon Street." It was at one of Harrington's crusades in 1969 that Baird got back on track and was inspired to start a ministry of his own.[10]

By the time Baird met Annie Yarborough, he had been traveling the United States and South America for seven years. After attending a race at Cale Yarborough's invitation, Baird was still indifferent toward the sport, but he felt a quick connection to some of NASCAR's statesmen, namely Yarborough, Richard Petty, Darrell Waltrip, and Benny Parsons.

In the same way Bobby Allison supported Frazier, the veteran driver also took a liking to Baird. He appreciated his down-to-earth approach and friendly demeanor. Allison also felt comfortable that the six-foot-five, 265-pound chaplain could fend for himself in a pinch.

"Bill was a big man," Allison says. "He had a great personality. Bill Frazier had a good personality too, I thought, but Bill Baird was probably more outgoing. He was hard not to pay attention to because he was one of those kinds of people that drew attention. It was great for his ministry. Anybody who wasn't happy about him being there knew they'd have trouble if they wanted to physically remove him."[11]

Even with that level of support, Baird's tenure got off to a slow start. Chapel attendance had dwindled in the two years prior to his arrival, and it took a while for the rest of the garage to get behind him.

"Not too many of them came to church, but they tolerated me," Baird once said. "They just wanted to make sure I wasn't some kind of leech. Once they saw I wasn't trying to take anything from them and actually liked them, they started coming around. I tried to start doing things for drivers, too. Sometimes you need to offer more than a prayer."[12]

When Baird created an interdenominational ministry called "Chapel 500," several drivers asked their fan clubs for donations, but that effort fell well short of what Baird and his family needed. So Benny Parsons called a drivers' meeting and took up an impromptu offering that laid the groundwork for future support.[13]

Like his predecessor, Baird often used the scorers' stands as his church. He also continued the tradition of praying for drivers and their teams on pit road just before the start of each race.[14] But Baird brought some new ideas too, such as an early service for wives and families, and a drivers' relief fund that also assisted crew members.[15]

In 1983 Phil Parsons, Benny's little brother, debuted at the Daytona 500, but he had been around the sport for much longer than that. When Benny moved from Detroit to North Carolina in 1970, the younger Parsons would spend his summers as a teenager and young adult hanging out at his brother's shop and behind the scenes at the track. He remembers Bill Frazier being around the garage area, and he even vaguely recalls seeing the old mobile chapel.[16]

But his relationship with Baird ran much deeper. In fact, Baird baptized Parsons after he became a Christian, and he also officiated the wedding of Parsons and his wife, Marcia. At that point in the sport's history, he says that ministry at the track was old hat, and much of that reality was due to some key leadership.

"Darrell [Waltrip] would come to mind," Parsons says. "Richard [Petty] was also involved. He was and is The King. That certainly showed that it was acceptable. When The King endorses or is part of something, then it's okay."[17]

Mass Appeal

On February 18, 1979, CBS became the first network to broadcast a five-hundred-mile NASCAR event from start to finish. It just so happened to be the Daytona 500, and it just so happened to feature one of the most memorable endings in stock car racing history. Just over fifteen million people watched as Richard Petty avoided a wreck between Cale Yarborough and Donnie Allison on the last lap and captured the checkered flag in the process.[18]

But it wasn't Petty's victory that viewers were talking about the next morning as much as the fight that broke out in the infield grass between Yarborough, Allison, and his brother, Bobby Allison. Exactly nine months later, Petty would have the last laugh by winning his record seventh championship.[19]

It is widely believed that the 1979 Daytona 500 was one of the most important races in NASCAR's history. For the first time, a mass audience was taking a look at stock car racing as a legitimate contender for its collective attention.

At the same time, NASCAR's inner circle was getting more comfortable with its latest ministry representative. That included Bobby Allison, who quietly was having perhaps an equal amount of influence on Baird's success as he did with Frazier's. Ironically, Allison rarely benefited from the existence of on-site chapel, due to his Catholic beliefs. Instead, he always opted to attend mass on the Saturday night before a race or early on a Sunday morning.

Allison was raised in a devout Catholic family along with nine brothers and sisters. After graduating from Curley High School in Miami, Florida, he moved to Wisconsin to live with an aunt and uncle and take a job working at the Ford Motor Company proving grounds, a place where new vehicles are developed and tested. In reality, Allison's mother was trying to get him away from racing, but much to her chagrin, there were racetracks all across the state with races taking place seemingly every day of the week.

Allison eventually moved back to Florida, but he quickly found the racing scene in the neighboring state of Alabama to be more lucrative. He and his brother Donnie set up shop in Hueytown and became known as "The Alabama Gang." There, Allison worked as a mechanic and engine tester before trying his hand behind the wheel.

After racing in the 1961 Daytona 500 (along with three other races for Ralph Stark that year) and winning a 1962 national championship in the modified special division, Allison worked his way up to the Grand National Series in 1965 for eight races followed by a thirty-three-race schedule in 1966.

But no matter what the circumstance, he always made sure to find a church in the area where he could attend mass. This certainly was the case on May 24, 1981, the morning of the World 600. At seven o'clock that morning, Allison arrived at St. Peter's in downtown Charlotte along with a very small handful of parishioners.

An elderly priest, Father Sebastian, then came out and said, "I need an altar boy."

"I served mass at my parents' fiftieth wedding anniversary, but other than that, I had not been an altar boy," Allison recalls. "So I didn't volunteer. There were a couple other men there, but nobody spoke up."

The priest then turned to Allison.

"I said, I need an altar boy," he firmly repeated.

Clearly being put on the spot, Allison did his best to respectfully reply.

"Father, I have not served," he said. "I am not an altar boy, but I will do whatever you want me to do."

Allison served for Father Sebastian and then headed back to the track, where he won his second career World 600 and the first since 1971. The following year, Allison returned to that same church on the morning of the race. With about twenty people in attendance, Father Sebastian walked out and gave the crowd a short address.

"A year ago, I needed a server, and a young man served for me," he said. "I understand he then won that big race."

Allison was quick to stand up and identify himself as the winning driver.

"I'm back again, Father," he replied. "And I'll serve again if you want me to."[20]

Small Group, Big Impact

Throughout the 1980s NASCAR continued to grow. The groundwork that legends such as Richard Petty and Bobby Allison had laid during the 1960s and 1970s was paying off in spades. An economic boom certainly didn't hurt as corporations were increasingly viewing the sport as a safe bet for product placement and successful marketing campaigns.

In 1982 the Late Model Sportsman Division was changed to the NASCAR Busch Series (now the Nationwide Series) as a reflection of its new sponsor. On July 4, 1984, Petty won his record-setting two-hundreth career (and final) race at the Firecracker 400 hosted by the Daytona International Speedway.[21] Petty's milestone was further etched into the history books by the fact that Ronald Reagan became the first sitting U.S. president to attend a NASCAR event. Petty climbed through the grandstands and into the press box, where he enjoyed a brief conversation with the president.

As Petty approached the twilight of his career, Darrell Waltrip was still in his prime. Waltrip and his close friend Lake Speed were also coming into their own as spiritual leaders in the garage. Waltrip had been around since 1972, while Speed had entered the scene in 1980.

In 1982 an eighteen-year-old hotshot from Texas made his NASCAR debut at North Wilkesboro, host of the Northwestern

Bank 400. Bobby Hillin Jr. raced five times that summer with legendary crew chief Henry Hyde before returning to finish his senior year at Midland High School. Over the next two seasons, Hillin steadily increased his race load until 1985, when he started twenty-eight races, followed by a full season of twenty-nine races in 1986. On July 27 Hillin collected his first and only Cup victory at the Talladega 500.

During that time, Hillin sporadically attended chapel service, but, as was the case with many of the drivers, he went with less-than-pure motives.

"It was kind of like an insurance policy," Hillin says. "You think if you go to chapel service, maybe God is going to smile on you. I don't believe in that today, but before I was a Christian, that was my mindset."[22]

Firmly settled into the NASCAR culture, Hillin eventually moved into a condominium that was down the hall from Lake Speed and Speed's wife. The seemingly innocuous circumstance turned out to be a game changer.

"I was kind of a wild man," Hillin admits. "Lake and his wife were pretty different. They would always invite me to dinner, and then they'd pull that Bible out, and they'd start reading it to me. I knew whenever they asked me to come over to dinner, they were going to be reading that Bible. I wanted a good meal, so I let them read it to me."[23]

Speed didn't just invite Hillin over for dinner, but he also asked him to join his wife and the Waltrips for Bible studies on the road. In 1985 Hillin was again asked to join them at a meeting in one of the hotel rooms. He sheepishly agreed to attend after having dinner with his crew, but he had no intentions of following through. As it turns out, Hillin's hotel room was next to the room where the Bible study was being held. The small group had the doors and windows open, and Hillin had no choice but to walk by them.

"Bobby, come on in!" one of them shouted.

"My heart was beating pretty fast," Hillin recalls. "But I ended up going in. By the end of the night, I had prayed to receive Christ."[24]

A New Direction

While Bill Baird was handling the typical chaplain duties, Waltrip, Speed, and a newlywed Hillin, along with their wives, continued meeting each week at the racetrack, usually in one of their motor coaches on a Friday or Saturday. A few months later, Phil and Marcia Parsons joined the group.

According to Parsons, Baird "became a little erratic" and wasn't there every week.[25] By 1987, the small Bible study group was feeling the need to start looking elsewhere for spiritual leadership. That year at Riverside, a pastor, Max Helton, invited Waltrip, Speed, and Hillin to speak at his church earlier in the race week. Helton then attended the race on Sunday.[26]

"[My wife] Stevie was in the car reading a book, and [Max] came over and pecked on the window and asked if he could visit with her," Waltrip says. "He told her that the Lord had called him to move back East and start a racing ministry. We were blown away because this is what we'd been praying."[27]

For a brief time, Helton was loosely involved in ministry at the track where he led the Waltrip group's Bible study. And then one Sunday, Baird asked Helton to preach the Sunday chapel sermon.

"Fairly soon after that, Bill Baird was no longer around, and Max was more or less our official chaplain," Parsons explains.[28]

By 1988, Helton and his family had moved to North Carolina. Waltrip formally introduced him to NASCAR president Bill France Jr., along with Dick Beatty and Les Richter. "This is the guy we want to represent us a chaplain," Waltrip told them.

"As long as the drivers want you here, we want you here," they replied.[29]

Thus, Motor Racing Outreach (MRO) was formed.

"That was the beginning of what we have today," Waltrip says. "Everybody loved Max. He was a great guy, a great teacher. He walked up and down the coach lot, and he'd knock on the door, come in and sit down and ask for some ice cream, or he'd ask what was going on or if he could pray with you. He created what he called a hangout ministry. At the track you just hang out. His vision was that when you're at the track, you just hang out with the guys, and when you have the opportunity, you give a profession of faith or talk about the Lord."[30]

Helton remained the president of MRO until 2002, when he left to create another racing ministry, World Span. According to NASCAR historian Buz McKim, Helton was the one who "made ministry at the track really stick."[31] Former crew chief and current television broadcaster Larry McReynolds concurs and describes Helton as "the salt of the earth."[32]

Helton passed away in 2008, but his impact on the sport had long since been felt and was especially key during the late 1980s and through the 1990s.

"MRO just took off and grew," Hillin says. "A lot of the drivers who were going to the chapel services like I had been, as that insurance policy, they started to accept Christ as their personal savior. It was a pretty incredible time of spiritual growth."[33]

Star Power

Just like when Bill Frazier and Bill Baird entered the scene, the initial success of MRO hinged upon the support of NASCAR's racing community, especially that of the drivers and their families. Darrell Waltrip continued to be the driving force behind Max Helton's efforts to continue the tradition of on-site ministry. Waltrip wouldn't have acknowledged his own contributions at the time, but certainly he was more aware of them a few years down the road. When Waltrip was inducted into the 2012 class of the NASCAR Hall of Fame, he mentioned in his acceptance speech that helping MRO get off the ground was among the things for which he was the proudest.[34]

For those within the sport, Waltrip was one of the least likely to provide the foundation for such a well-respected ministry. Early in his career, he admits, he was more interested in promoting himself than promoting Jesus, and it took a violent wreck during the 1983 Daytona 500 for him to get his priorities straightened out.

"It was a wake-up call," Waltrip says. "I'm not anywhere near the same guy I was then. It put some humility back in me. It took the focus off of myself, which is where it had been, and it softened my heart and let me look at people differently. It was a changing of my heart."[35]

Waltrip wasn't immediately transformed into a saint-like figure, nor would he claim to be at that level in his faith today. In fact, he was still known throughout the 1980s for some explosive on-the-track feuds, including a well-chronicled ongoing battle with Dale Earnhardt.

"What I loved about Darrell is that he was willing to set himself up," former Cup chaplain Dale Beaver says. "He might be reading Scriptures in chapel one minute, and then he's out there on the racetrack getting wrecked and ready to whip Ricky Craven. Darrell set himself up like [the apostle] Peter would. Darrell was a lot like Peter. I loved that about him."[36]

Over the next few years, Cup regulars such as Mark Martin, Dale Jarrett, Kyle Petty, Bobby Labonte, and Jeff Gordon made public professions of faith. They were also among the growing list of drivers willing to use their star power in an effort to promote MRO.

"It was becoming more normal," Ned Jarrett says. "A bigger percentage of them were attending the services, and they were supporting it financially to help it continue on and to grow. I did not see them getting up on a stump and preaching about it. If it came about in a conversation or in an interview with the press, many of them would take the opportunity to talk about the ministry and how they felt and that they believed in God and how it helped them to continue on in the sport when some of the [tragic] things happened."[37]

Martin was a particularly interesting case. In many ways he was (and remains) somewhat of a throwback to the quiet but tough drivers from 1940s and 1950s. Martin debuted at the 1981 Northwestern Bank 400 at North Wilkesboro, but he didn't solidify himself as a star until his first win at Rockingham, host of the 1989 AC Delco 500. After his good friend Clifford Allison was killed in 1992 during a practice session, Martin rededicated his life to Christ.[38]

Since that time, Martin has often allowed his testimony to be used in outreach efforts, but he admittedly had never been comfortable with being as vocal about his faith as Waltrip and others who had more outgoing personalities.

"I don't think that I'm the smartest guy around," Martin says in his typical self-deprecating fashion. "So I'm better off to keep my mouth shut as much as I can rather than opening my mouth and proving to people that I don't know what I'm talking about. I'm more of a leader by example than I am a preacher."[39]

Tim Griffin, who served as the lead Cup chaplain from 2005 to 2011, observed Martin's approach to ministry later in the popular driver's career.

"I think Mark decided there are things he can do very well, and that's what he was going to focus on," Griffin says. "When it comes to how Mark lives out his faith, there's no doubt he has seen the opportunity that he has to model what a person under the control of another influence—in this case his faith in God—can manifest in his life. He's one of those guys that you're not going to see lose his cool. You're not going to see him shoot off his mouth. He's going to live at peace with his neighbor. He's going to try to live out his faith, and I think he's given himself to God's control in his life to where his platform is going to be established by what he does and not necessarily just a bunch of words that fly out of his mouth. That's just not who he is."[40]

The Ringer

Motorsports historians often point toward the 1992 season finale at Atlanta Motor Speedway as one of the most significant races in NASCAR history. At the time, it was celebrated as Richard Petty's final race—the conclusion of an unmatched thirty-five-year career. The Hooters 500 eventually would become equally known for being the Cup Series debut of a twenty-one-year old driver named Jeff Gordon.[41]

But for NASCAR ministry (and in particular MRO), one of the most noteworthy events took place nine months earlier at the Daytona 500 when Joe Gibbs Racing (JGR) debuted at the Cup level with a young Dale Jarrett in the now iconic #18 car. Jarrett, son of legendary driver Ned Jarrett, finished in thirty-fifth place after an accident took him out of contention.

Just like Gordon's appearance on the scene, no one could know for sure the impact that the Washington Redskins head coach would have on NASCAR over the next two decades. But even before the green flag was dropped at Daytona, there was a pretty good idea of how influential Joe Gibbs was going to be as a spiritual leader.

It all started on a spring day in 1991 when Interstate Batteries CEO Norm Miller received an unusual phone call. His secretary informed him that Gibbs was on the line, but Miller immediately brushed it off as a practical joke by one of his friends.

"And then I picked up the phone, and it was really Joe," he laughingly says.[42]

Miller had already been using motorsports as an advertising vehicle for his company. Interstate Batteries cofounded the Great American Race, a cross-country antique car event that ran from 1983 through 1996. Miller also sponsored a driver, Stanley Smith, in the All-American Series.

After recovering from the shock of Gibbs's call, Miller set up a meeting for the two of them to meet in Dallas. Miller discovered that MRO president Max Helton had suggested that Gibbs approach him about a new racing team. Although Gibbs was still the Redskins head coach, he was looking for a new venture to pursue during his impending retirement from the National Football League (NFL).

Miller was immediately intrigued. Not only had he experienced marketing success in the motorsports world, but he also liked the idea of partnering with a fellow Christian.

"When we first met, I told them that, at that stage in my life, I didn't want to do anything that was going to occupy my time if I didn't think we could lift up Christ doing it," Miller says. "He told me I'd hit his button right on the money. We locked hearts at the time. You don't make a whole lot of close friends after you're fifty or sixty years old, but we did."[43]

It turned out to be a banner year for Gibbs. Not only did he secure sponsorship funding for his racing team, but also he led Washington to the NFL playoffs and ultimately a spot in Super Bowl XXIV on January 27, 1992. The night before the big game, Miller and some of the JGR personnel joined Gibbs and his team at a joint chapel service. At the conclusion of Tom Skinner's message, the team's crew chief, Jimmy Makar, prayed to receive Christ. His wife, Patty, who is Dale Jarrett's sister, along with Dale and his wife, Kelly, recommitted their lives to the faith.[44]

As far as Miller was concerned, Washington's 37–24 victory over the Buffalo Bills was icing on the cake for what had already been a momentous two days in Minnesota. With the Daytona 500 just three weeks away, he was energized and excited about what the 1992 Cup season had in store.

Gibbs and Miller knew that they were the new guys entering a tightly knit racing community. To rectify the situation, they decided to have a dinner at Daytona ahead of the race that would double as an outreach event for MRO. They rented a hotel ballroom, brought in Ricky Skaggs to entertain the guests, and utilized Darrell Waltrip as the master of ceremonies. At the end, Gibbs shared his testimony with the six hundred people in attendance, including crews, families, media, and NASCAR officials.[45]

The event was successful on both accounts. It helped Joe Gibbs Racing enter the sport with a splash, but more important to Gibbs and Miller was the dinner's spiritual results. An estimated forty people accepted Christ for the first time, while 160 more recommitted their lives to God. In the immediate aftermath, Sunday chapel services doubled in size.[46]

In the long term, members of the NASCAR family were able to enjoy and learn from a steady, consistent example of what it looks like to dedicate one's life to the Lord.

"Joe Gibbs is the embodiment of somebody that really cares," MRO president Billy Mauldin says. "He can be intense as a competitor and a coach. He wants to win. He enjoys winning like anybody else. But in pursuing that, he cares about people and everybody knows it. That's not just human character. That's the Christlikeness in him that allows a sense of love and true caring and concern to come out within the community. There's a high level of respect for Joe. People know he's the real deal."[47]

Gibbs wasn't instantly accepted and admired just by the insiders. He quickly became a popular figure within the NASCAR fan base as well. According to Dr. Roger Marsh, Gibbs has taken that same evangelistic mindset and translated it to successful Raceway Ministries–sponsored outreaches in the camping areas.

"Joe has been really good about coming out to our displays and hanging out with the fans and showing off Super Bowl rings," Marsh says. "When the fans see Joe Gibbs, they light up. They're attracted to him, not only because he's a winner but also because they know what he stands for and they respect that highly."[48]

But just as soon as Gibbs and his team had buoyed spiritual growth in the garage and beyond, tumultuous times around the corner were about to test everyone's faith.

NOTES

1. NASCAR, *2013 NASCAR Media Guide* (NASCAR Integrated Marketing Communications), 29.
2. Dr. Roger Marsh, interview with the author, February 17, 2012.
3. Todd Deaton, "Gentlemen, Start Your Engines," *The Courier*, May 23, 2006 (http://baptistcourier.com/2006/05/gentlemen-start-your-engines-2/).
4. Dr. Roger Marsh, interview with the author, February 7, 2013.
5. Deaton, "Gentlemen, Start Your Engines."
6. Dr. Roger Marsh, interview with the author, February 7, 2013.
7. Dr. Roger Marsh, interview with the author, February 17, 2012.
8. Tom Archdeacon, "And Then the Lord Sent Brother Bill," *Miami News*, July 3, 1981.
9. Ibid.
10. Ibid.
11. Bobby Allison, interview with the author, February 14, 2012.
12. Archdeacon, "And Then the Lord Sent Brother Bill."
13. Joyce Leviton, "Stock Car Preacher Bill Baird Brings Uplift to the Tracks but No Talk of Hellfire or Dying," *People* 13, no. 23 (June 1980).
14. Ibid.
15. Archdeacon, "And Then the Lord Sent Brother Bill."
16. Phil Parsons, interview with the author, December 11, 2012.
17. Ibid.
18. NASCAR, *2013 NASCAR Media Guide*, 29.
19. Ibid.
20. Bobby Allison, interview with the author, February 14, 2012.
21. NASCAR, *2013 NASCAR Media Guide*, 29.
22. Bobby Hillin Jr., interview with the author, February 10, 2012.
23. Ibid.
24. Ibid.
25. Phil Parsons, interview with the author, December 11, 2012.
26. Bobby Hillin Jr., interview with the author, February 10, 2012.
27. Darrell Waltrip, interview with the author, October 2, 2010.

28. Phil Parsons, interview with the author, December 11, 2012.
29. Darrell Waltrip, interview with the author, October 2, 2010.
30. Ibid.
31. Buz McKim, interview with the author, January 31, 2012.
32. Larry McReynolds, interview with the author, October 2, 2010.
33. Bobby Hillin Jr., interview with the author, February 10, 2012.
34. Buz McKim, interview with the author, January 31, 2012.
35. Darrell Waltrip, "I Looked at What I Had Accomplished and What I
    Had Won, and Realized There Was No Glory There," *Beyond the Ultimate*
    (http://www.beyondtheultimate.org/athlete/Darrell-Waltrip).
36. Dale Beaver, interview with the author, August 21, 2012.
37. Ned Jarrett, interview with the author, August 21, 2012.
38. Mark Martin, "Mark Martin's Christian Testimony,"
    http://www.go2mro.com/testimonies/markmartin.php.
39. Mark Martin, interview with the author, October 28, 2008.
40. Tim Griffin, interview with the author, November 5, 2008.
41. NASCAR, *2013 NASCAR Media Guide*, 30.
42. Norm Miller, interview with the author, August 21, 2012.
43. Ibid.
44. Ibid.
45. Ibid.
46. Ibid.
47. Billy Mauldin, interview with the author, December 5, 2011.
48. Dr. Roger Marsh, interview with the author, February 17, 2012.

CHAPTER 5

Death and Life

NASCAR drivers have long accepted the fact that serious injury and even death is a possibility that exists every time they maneuver into their cars and start their engines. Over time, the injuries have become less severe, and the fatalities have become virtually nonexistent.

But even as technological advances helped make the sport safer, the twenty-year period that stretched from 1980 to 2000 remained extremely volatile and was dotted with unfortunate tragedies. In the 1980s alone, thirteen drivers were killed during practice sessions, qualifying laps, or races throughout the various divisions, including five deaths at the Cup level.

That number could have easily been upped to six had it not been for the presence of ESPN pit reporter Dr. Jerry Punch. On August 26, 1988, the drivers were engaged in a Friday afternoon practice session at Bristol Motor Speedway when Rusty Wallace wrecked and barrel-rolled down the front stretch. Punch was first to arrive at the scene of Wallace's crash and immediately recognized that the driver was unconscious and not breathing. An emergency room physician before his broadcasting days, Punch revived Wallace, who would recover in time to start the Busch 500 the following night.

"You don't think about what could have happened until later when you sit back and look at the details of what would have happened had we not been able to get an airway open for him," Punch says. "We feel very blessed. I always look back and tell Rusty that after that happened I had so many drivers, like Dale Earnhardt, who were friends with Rusty that said, 'You saved Rusty's life? Why? Why would you do that?' We'd all laugh about it jokingly, just picking on Rusty. But we were fortunate that it happened that way."[1]

Three months later in Atlanta, Punch saved Automobile Racing Club of America (ARCA) driver Don Marmor's life after a vicious crash during the Atlanta Journal 500K, and he would do the same for Ernie Irvin six years later following a practice session crash at Michigan International Speedway. Subsequent stories would, unfortunately, not have the benefit of a happy ending.

Modern-Day Job

In 1987 Bobby Allison was enjoying his twenty-fourth year as a NASCAR driver. He wasn't the same dominant force as he was when he won ten races each in consecutive 1971 and 1972 seasons, or even as consistent as he was four years earlier in 1983 when he won six races en route to his sole Cup championship. But as he traveled to Talladega for the Winston 500 in May, Allison was still one of the sport's biggest names and a threat to crack the top ten at any given track.

After just twenty-one laps, Allison cut a tire, began to spin out, and went airborne while traveling over two hundred miles per hour. His rear bumper hit the protective catch fence just in front of the grandstands. The impact violently spun him around and caused the car to crash near the start-finish line.

Miraculously, Allison survived with no major injuries. His wreck, however, did bring on significant changes and has commonly been considered to be the event that caused NASCAR to start rethinking its safety policies for the superspeedways. That same year, officials mandated a smaller carburetor for the remaining races at Talladega and Daytona. The following year, NASCAR instituted the required use of restrictor plates[2] at those two tracks.

But Allison was undaunted by what had happened in Talladega and saw no need to think twice about getting back into his car.

"I was so optimistic about racing," Allison says. "I loved it to the point that every time I had a crash, I thought that was the last crash I'd ever have. So I went back to going as wide open as I could go."[3]

Allison finished the balance of the season and prepared for the 1988 race schedule like always. On February 14 NASCAR ran its first Daytona 500 with the mandated use of restrictor plates—a direct result of Allison's Talladega wreck nine months earlier. It was a change that suited Allison well. He won his third career Daytona 500 and celebrated in Victory Lane with his son Davey, who had completed the historic one-two, father-son finish.

On June 19 the Cup Series traveled to Pocono International Speedway, where Allison had won three times in twenty-one attempts. But when he reported a flat tire just before the green flag dropped, it seemed as if his day would be doomed from the start. Allison tried to complete the first lap before heading to his pit for a tire change, but he never made it back. Driving into the infamous tunnel turn, Allison slammed the outside wall and was hit hard by Jocko Maggiacomo in his driver's-side door.

Geoff Bodine went on to win the Miller High Life 500 at Pocono that day, but the day would become better remembered as the race that ended Allison's career due to massive head injuries that essentially erased his recollection of his special moment with son Davey at the 1988 Daytona 500.

"It was really tough," Allison says. "I healed up from the physical injuries quickly and incredibly well, but my head injury gave me terrible memory loss. I would see somebody who had been a good friend, and I wouldn't know them. I was dealing with a lot of confusion."[4]

Allison didn't stay out of the game for long. In 1990 he reentered the scene as a team owner. Although his memory issues persisted, Allison was still able to run the shop while simultaneously enjoying his two sons' racing careers.

By 1992, Allison's older son, Davey, had already won thirteen Cup races and was on the verge of another great season. It all started on February 16, when Davey held off Morgan Shepherd to win the Daytona 500. With the win, Bobby and Davey Allison became the second father-son duo (behind Lee and Richard Petty) to win NASCAR's most famous race. Davey would finish the season with five Cup victories and his second consecutive third-place finish in the standings.

Clifford Allison, on the other hand, was just starting his third season in the Busch Series. On August 13 the twenty-seven-year old driver was taking laps during a practice session at Michigan International Speedway when he lost control of his car between the third and fourth turns and hit the concrete wall on the driver's side. Allison died of severe trauma on the way to the hospital.[5]

"It was an incredible tragedy," Bobby Allison says. "I can't even put it into perspective from my standpoint. I wasn't mentally recovered enough to be able to deal with it like I could have had I not been injured at Pocono. It was so devastating to me. It caused me so much mental agony on a constant basis. Somebody would walk up and say something, and I'd start crying. It was a terrible, terrible deal."[6]

Larry McReynolds had become very close to the Allison family during the 1990s. He was Davey Allison's crew chief in 1992, when Allison won the Daytona 500 in the #28 car. After Clifford's death, McReynolds and team owner Robert Yates were finally able to connect with Davey in Michigan. They were beside themselves and didn't know what to do next.

"Do you want us to find somebody to drive the Cup car?" McReynolds recalls asking Allison.

"Let me tell you guys something," he replied. "Yes, I'm devastated over my brother being killed today, but I'm here to do a job, and I'm going to do my job. I'm going to do the job the best I can."

"Think about it," McReynolds says. "That weekend, he had to drive through that same corner where his brother was killed."[7]

Over the remaining three months of the season, both Bobby and son Davey trudged along in their respective responsibilities as owner and driver. For the elder Allison, spending time with his son became therapeutic, and the two regularly traveled together to different events. But just as he felt himself regaining control of his scattered emotions, tragedy struck the family again.

Davey Allison was having another solid year. After sixteen races, he had notched another Cup victory and eight top-ten finishes. He was also a skilled pilot and had become accustomed to flying his own plane to many of the racetracks.

It was July 12, 1993, when Allison flew his newly acquired helicopter to Talladega to watch Cup driver and close friend Neil Bonnett help his son David Bonnett test a car for an upcoming Busch Series debut. Along the way, Allison picked up former driver and family friend Red Farmer and headed to the track.

According to witness reports, the helicopter was within a foot of touching down when suddenly it shot up about twenty-five feet, spun counterclockwise, and then hit the ground and began to roll. By the time the aircraft had come to a stop, onlookers were already attempting to rescue the two men. Farmer was pulled out first, followed by an unconscious Allison.[8]

On July 13, just sixteen hours after the crash, Davey Allison died of massive head injuries. Farmer lived to recall the horrific circumstances that took another child away from Bobby and Judy Allison. In a fateful twist, Davey Allison died just eleven months, to the day, after Clifford was killed in Michigan.

"When we lost Davey, it put me right back into such a feeling of being totally defeated," Bobby Allison says. "It was mental and physical pain that you can't believe. The one thing that I could do is I could pray."[9]

For McReynolds, Davey's death was a particularly bitter pill to swallow.

"I've always said that Davey Allison was not only my best friend, but he was my role model as a man of faith and how to stay strong when you think there's no way you can take any more," he explains. "Davey had a little saying. It was simply, 'There is nothing that can come my way today that God and I can't handle together.' If there was anybody who lived by that saying, it was Davey Allison."[10]

Over a span of just twelve months, Bobby Allison and his family had experienced an unparalleled amount of difficulty. Often referred to as a modern-day Job, the long-suffering Bible character, Allison relied heavily on his faith to overcome the immense pain. But within three years of Davey's death, the sum total of those tragic events had taken its toll.

"Judy and I were disagreeing about everything," Allison says. "If she said the sky is pretty, I'd say, 'No, it isn't. It's cloudy.' We argued about everything. We just both were so distraught over the loss of both of our boys in that eleven-month period. Finally, we decided to go our separate ways. It was just one of those situations that we dealt with."[11]

A Royal Tragedy

The 1994 season was bookended by two very different historic events. On February 11 Neil Bonnett was taking part in the first practice session for the Daytona 500. Heading into the fourth turn, he lost control of his car after his right front tire went down. Bonnett hit the outside wall in a near head-on collision and died on impact.

The fatal accident was compounded by what happened three days later. During a subsequent practice session at Daytona, rookie driver Rodney Orr was making a mock qualifying run when his car spun out on the second turn. His car went airborne and slammed into the retaining wall and catch fence while traveling over 175 miles per hour. Like Bonnett, Orr was killed instantly.

Bonnett's and Orr's deaths were the first NASCAR fatalities to take place during the same event since June 1956, when Clint McHugh was killed during his qualifying lap at NASCAR's Grand National Division race in West Memphis, followed by Thomas "Cotton" Priddy, who died in the race the next day.

But on October 23, at Rockingham, the season struck a more celebratory tone when Dale Earnhardt clinched his seventh Cup title, placing him in a record-setting tie with Richard Petty.

In 1995 NASCAR launched the SuperTruck Series, which most recently has become known as the Camping World Truck Series. It was two years later, on March 16, 1997, that NASCAR experienced its next significant tragedy. At Homestead-Miami Speedway, John Nemechek, younger brother of Cup driver Joe Nemechek, suffered head trauma in an accident that took place during the Florida Dodge Dealers 400K. He died five days later at the age of twenty-seven.

Historically, NASCAR had also done its best to advance its safety measures for the drivers, but too often it found itself behind the curve. Fire-retardant suits, for instance, were not required until after Fireball Roberts died after complications of burns suffered in a flame-inducing crash at Charlotte Motor Speedway in 1964. It was Bobby Allison's nearly fatal accident in 1988 that caused NASCAR to get serious about the use of restrictor plates at all of its superspeedways, where two-hundred-mile-per-hour jaunts around the track were becoming commonplace.

But as the turn of the century approached, a series of unthinkable tragedies would result in an intense time of soul searching within the sport.

As NASCAR was celebrating its fiftieth anniversary during the 1998 season, Dale Beaver, a recent seminary graduate, was doing some soul searching of his own. Through a relationship with former Interstate Batteries corporate chaplain Jim Cody, Beaver was entertaining an intriguing offer to replace Max Helton as the lead chaplain for the Cup Series. Cody, then the Motor Racing Outreach (MRO) director of chaplaincy, told Beaver that he would train with Helton for a year and then take over his responsibilities.

Not long after Beaver's wife, Andree, gave birth to their second child, the couple went to Bristol for a race and the opportunity to observe MRO in action. It didn't take long for the young minister to see that this was where he was supposed to be.

"For some reason, God has given me a real ability to connect with people as a spiritual director and the pastoral component that goes along with that," Beaver explains. "People have always felt at ease with me. I don't know why I was given that ability, but it's what I've always been able to carry around with me. With that comes the ability to challenge people when they're off track and also identify the fact that I'm walking the same road that they're walking, and that I'm not any different than they are. I'm from a blue-collar background, but I'm white-collar trained. That's what it was like in NASCAR. You had these guys making millions of dollars. They had a white-collar experience from a blue-collar upbringing."[12]

As the 2000 season approached, Beaver was preparing for his second year on the job. At the same time, Adam Petty was preparing to make history as the Cup Series' first fourth-generation driver. Petty had already debuted at the Busch (now Nationwide) Series level in 1998 and was scheduled to run a limited Cup schedule in preparation for a full-time ride in 2001.

On April 2 Petty etched his name in NASCAR's record book when he qualified for the DirecTV 500 at Texas Motor Speedway and made his first Cup appearance. Lee Petty was able to watch his great-grandson's historic race, but he died three days later, at the age of eighty-six.

While Adam Petty was aiming toward his full-time Cup opportunity the following year, his focus in 2000 was learning the ropes in NASCAR's secondary division. On May 12 he was taking practice laps for the Busch 200 at the New Hampshire International Speedway in Loudon when an inexplicable mechanical malfunction caused his throttle to stick. Driving into the third turn, Petty lost control of his car and hit the outside wall head-on. He died instantly from a basilar skull fracture.

At the time of his death, Petty was nineteen years old, just two months from his twentieth birthday. His fatal crash sent chills throughout not just the NASCAR community, but the entire sports world. Furthermore, Petty was racing royalty. The hopes of an entire family had rested upon the young man's shoulders. And just like that, he was gone.

"I'll never forget when (MRO director of public affairs and community relations) Missy DeSouza called me," Beaver recalls. "I was in the parking lot of a Home Depot. She said, 'Dale, have you heard about Adam?' I immediately thought of my son Adam, who was seven years old at the time. But then she told me the news: Adam Petty had been killed at Loudon. I had to shake that off and immediately go be with this family because no one else was there to do that."[13]

To this day, Beaver can give a mile-by-mile account of his 90-minute drive from Charlotte to Randleman to see the Petty family. Still fairly new to the racing community, he had the unenviable task of telling Richard Petty that his grandson had died.

"I kept thinking, 'What am I doing here?'" Beaver says. "This was sacred hallowed ground with this family, and yet I was the guy who was supposed to be there at the time. That was a bit scary."[14]

For Beaver, it was like being a new pastor in town. He didn't know the family that well yet, but he had gotten to know Adam's father, Kyle, somewhat during preseason testing and at Daytona earlier in the year. More than anything, Beaver wanted to get to the Petty compound before they could hear about it on radio or through a television report.

As NASCAR continued to feel the effects of Petty's death, Bobby Allison was empathizing with his former rival. The legendary driver had been divorced for three years, but the day after the tragedy in Loudon he was at a wedding with his ex-wife, Judy. Both were there to support Davey's widow, who was getting remarried.

"As we were leaving the wedding, Judy said to me, 'We should put our differences aside and go try to help the Pettys,'" Allison remembers. "I thought that was such an incredibly strong, giving attitude. So I said, 'Definitely, we will.'"15

The next morning, they drove Judy's car to North Carolina and spent some significant time with the Petty family. It turned out to be a good thing for both parties involved.

"We felt like just being there would offer the comfort and the support that we were sure that they needed, because we knew how bad we needed it [when our sons died]," Allison says. "We felt so good that Richard, Lynda, Kyle, and Pattie appreciated us being there so much."16

As they drove back to Alabama, it became clear to both Bobby and Judy that it was time for them to move past their own hurts and reconcile. A few weeks later they remarried in a civil ceremony, and they have been together ever since.

The Double Rainbow

NASCAR had barely caught its breath when tragedy struck the sport once again. In fact, it was exactly eight weeks after Adam Petty's death, on July 7, when 1998 Winston Cup Rookie of the Year Kenny Irwin was practicing in Loudon, New Hampshire, for the New England 300.

Irwin was in his third full season at the Cup level and was still striving toward his first breakthrough performance. But off the track he was already one of the more liked drivers in the garage and had befriended Tony Stewart in particular.

During that Friday's practice session Irwin was heading into the third turn when his throttle got stuck. Unable to slow down, he hit the wall at 150 miles per hour and flipped onto his roof. Irwin, who likely was killed upon impact, crashed at almost the exact same spot where Adam Petty had died two months earlier. The mechanical failure of his car was also identical to what happened to Petty's car.

"I've never seen people in more shock than the track workers that day," Beaver says. "It was a surreal situation."[17]

The following day, MRO worked with NASCAR to hold a memorial service for Irwin, but many attendees couldn't help simultaneously reliving Petty's death. As the people left the service, they started to notice an incredible sight. A double rainbow had formed over the very spot where both accidents had taken place.

"There's no telling all the reasons," Beaver says. "But God was working in the lives of the people impacted by these tragic events."[18]

Unfortunately, Irwin's death wasn't the last tragedy of the season. On October 13, at Texas Motor Speedway, Tony Roper was competing in the Craftsman Truck Series O'Reilly 400. One of the series' original drivers, Roper attempted to pass Steve Grissom but was turned into Grissom's front bumper by another truck. Roper's vehicle veered sharply to the right and took a hard hit into the concrete wall. He died a day later.

The NASCAR organization and its fans were collectively left to wonder, could it get any worse than this?

The Secret Life of the Intimidator

By 2001, Richard Petty, although nine years retired, was still "The King." But Dale Earnhardt Sr. clearly was NASCAR's new ruling authority. Earnhardt had slowly worked his way onto the scene with a combined nine Cup starts in four seasons (1975–1978), driving for five different owners. At the age of twenty-eight, he caught on with one of those owners, Rod Osterlund, and raced twenty-seven times en route to 1979 Winston Cup Rookie of the Year honors. At the fall race in Richmond he started a string of 647 races that would lead him up to the 2001 season.

Along the way, Earnhardt became one of the most dominant racers in NASCAR history. He won six of his seven Cup titles in an incredible nine-year stretch that included three sets of back-to-back championships (1986–1987, 1990–1991, 1993–1994). His hard-nosed, aggressive style of racing earned him the nickname "The Intimidator." In fact, he had gotten the famous moniker during the 1987 season after spinning out Bill Elliott during the final segment of the Winston (now referred to as the All-Star Race) and maintaining control of his own car after being forced into the infield grass.

Feuds were commonplace during Earnhardt's era, and he often was in the middle of some entertaining ones. Elliott, Terry Labonte, Geoff Bodine, Jeff Gordon, and Rusty Wallace were among some of his well-documented adversaries.

But perhaps Earnhardt's most spirited rivalry was with Darrell Waltrip, who was frequently referred to by his own nickname, "Jaws," and whose brash personality always seemed to rub the Intimidator the wrong way. Of course, it always started with something that took place out on the track.

Take 1986 in Richmond, for instance, where Waltrip was in control of the race until Earnhardt pulled close enough to wreck the leader and his own car in the process. Waltrip was convinced that Earnhardt was trying to kill him.[19]

But other times, Waltrip seemed to be looking for trouble, such as after he won a race at North Wilkesboro and a reporter asked if he was going to start playing mind games with Earnhardt and team owner Richard Childress, as Waltrip had been known to do.

"I would put something in the papers," Waltrip said, "But I know those boys can't read."[20]

Strangely, it was actually Waltrip who helped Earnhardt break into racing by lending him one of his cars, and it was Earnhardt who got Waltrip back into a Cup ride in 1998 by asking the aging star to replace Steve Park for thirteen races, after Park was injured driving in the #1 Dale Earnhardt Incorporated (DEI) car.[21]

Waltrip often reminisces about the tense battles that started on the track and usually spilled over into the media. He's also quick to point out the less-publicized part of their relationship.

"We had our moments," Waltrip says with a mischievous grin. "I always like to say we were 'frienemies.' We were friends part of the time, and enemies part of the time. When we were friends, we were really good friends. When we were enemies, we were *good* enemies."[22]

"Darrell and Dale had this love-hate relationship," Larry McReynolds adds. "They had a lot of encounters on the racetrack, but trust me, they truly respected each other."[23]

Earnhardt also had a sense of humor that often caught people off guard. He had no problem using his gruff exterior and his mean reputation to his advantage. Dale Beaver became one of Earnhardt's "victims" during the 2000 season at Pocono. Lonnie Clouse, a fellow MRO minister, was planning a camping trip in a mountainous area nearby for teenage children of the drivers and crew chiefs.

Earnhardt's youngest daughter, Taylor, was one of the kids going on the excursion, but first she needed a permission slip signed by one of her parents. Beaver took the paper to Earnhardt's publicist, John Rhodes, and asked him to get it signed and returned later. But when he went back to Rhodes twenty minutes later to retrieve the document, Beaver noticed that it wasn't signed.

"He wants to see you," Rhodes matter-of-factly stated.

"He wants to see me?" Beaver uneasily repeated.

"Yeah, he's got some questions for you."

Beaver did his best to hide his nerves as he followed Rhodes to the black #3 hauler. In true Intimidator fashion, the narrow hallway was completely dark. As he stepped up into the lounge, Beaver was even more surprised to see Earnhardt sitting in the dark, eating an orange.

"Yes, sir, you wanted to see me," he asked.

"Yeah, come sit down," Earnhardt ordered.

"It was like I was some dude he didn't know, and I was some guy who wanted to take his daughter away for the weekend," Beaver says. "It wasn't the best situation for me."

For the next minute or two Earnhardt sternly asked Beaver some tough questions. After making the chaplain sweat a little bit, he finally broke character.

"I'm gonna let her go," he laughed. "I just wanted to razz you a bit!"

After Beaver's heart rate finally slowed back to its normal pace, he was able to enjoy a memorable conversation with Earnhardt. The two identified as fathers while telling each other about their families.[24]

"It probably would surprise a lot of people, but there was a side to Dale that he kept to himself," Waltrip says. "He didn't want anybody to think he was a softie. He was the Intimidator, but there was a side to him that he didn't let a lot of people see."[25]

Andy Petree was one of a handful of people who saw firsthand the secret life of the Intimidator. Petree was Earnhardt's crew chief from 1993 to 1996 and was a part of the team's sixth and seventh Cup championships (1993, 1994). But even after leaving Richard Childress Racing to pursue a quieter life, albeit as a car owner, Petree and his wife would occasionally spend vacations together with the Earnhardts.

"I was really close friends with Dale even after I left," he says. "We spent some quality time away from everything. He was totally different. I got a kick out of seeing that other side of him. He was a great father. His daughter Taylor was young at the time. He'd run out into the surf and pull her around on a little raft. He did these things you'd never think the Intimidator would ever do. He was such a great host. He always wanted to make sure we had everything we needed. He was a very caring person. A lot of people never saw that."[26]

Earnhardt also had a soft spot for people in need. After his death, stories began to trickle out into the public square. One in particular stands out to NASCAR historian Buz McKim.

"There was a church not far from his shop that had a fundraiser to get their parking lot paved," he says. "One day, Earnhardt saw the preacher out there and asked him what he needed to pave his parking lot. The preacher told him how much. Earnhardt wrote him a check on the spot, but it was under one condition: The pastor couldn't tell anyone where the money came from."[27]

Earnhardt was never known to stick around for chapel service after the Sunday morning drivers' meeting, but he did develop an interesting ritual late in his career. It all started with something that Darrell Waltrip and his wife, Stevie, had been doing for a while. Before every race Stevie would write a Bible verse on a sticky note and put it on her husband's roll bar. Every race she would write a different verse that she hoped would provide him with strength, comfort, and inspiration.

No one remembers the exact date or race when it happened, but sometime during the late 1990s, Waltrip and Earnhardt qualified by each other. As they were standing outside the car on pit road before the race, Earnhardt saw Stevie put the sticky note inside Darrell's car.

"What the hell is that?" Earnhardt crassly asked.

"It's a Bible verse," she replied.

"Man, I'd like to have one of those," he said.

So from that moment on, Stevie would write up two Bible verses—one for her husband's car and one for Earnhardt's car.[28]

"My wife and he had a great relationship," Waltrip says. "She prayed with Dale. Dale and I also prayed together a lot. We were competitors, and we competed against each other as hard as anybody could compete, but we still had a great deal of respect for each other."[29]

Death and Life

When Waltrip retired at the end of the 2000 season, Earnhardt was concerned that he might not get his pre-race Bible verse anymore. But with her husband sticking around to work in the broadcast booth for Fox Sports, Stevie remained present, and assured Earnhardt that she would continue the sticky-note tradition.

On February 18, 2001, Stevie walked out to pit road and put a verse inside Earnhardt's car. It was Proverbs 18:10: "The name of the Lord is a strong tower and a rock. The righteous will run to it and be safe."[30]

Earnhardt qualified seventh for the race and was seeking just his second Daytona 500 victory. He had won the iconic event for the first time just three years earlier. Earnhardt wasn't just thinking about how his team might fare. He was also contemplating the potential success of his DEI racing partners—son Dale Earnhardt Jr., driving in the #8 car, and Darrell Waltrip's younger brother, Michael, driving in the newly formed #15 car.

While there was plenty of hard racing and exciting moments throughout, the 2001 Daytona 500 was relatively free of major incident until lap 173, when Robby Gordon and Ward Burton collided coming out of the second turn onto the back straightaway. In the aftermath, Tony Stewart was turned into the wall and pushed airborne over Gordon's car. Stewart violently flipped twice before coming to a stop on the infield grass. When the dust settled, eighteen cars had been knocked out of the race.

After a lengthy cleanup and several caution laps, the race resumed on lap 180. Waltrip led the pack to the restart and quickly got involved in a back-and-forth battle with Sterling Marlin. To everyone's amazement, Waltrip was trailed by teammates Earnhardt Jr. and Earnhardt Sr. heading into the final lap. By then, Marlin had been shuffled back to fourth place and was desperately trying to get past Earnhardt Sr.'s #3 car.

On the fourth turn, Marlin made contact with the Intimidator's left rear and caused him to slide off the steep banking and onto the flat apron. Earnhardt tried to correct course and turned sharply toward the outside retaining wall. As he worked to avoid slamming into the wall, his car crossed paths with Ken Schrader's #36 Pontiac. Schrader hit Earnhardt just behind the passenger door and pushed his car toward the wall. Earnhardt hit the wall head-on at an estimated speed of 160 miles per hour.

From the view of the grandstand and those watching on television, Earnhardt's crash didn't look terribly brutal. But when Schrader got out of his car to check on his fellow competitor, he knew instantly that Earnhardt was gone—although he wouldn't admit as much until ten years had passed.

"I didn't want to be the one who said, 'Dale is dead,'" Schrader told NASCAR.com reporter Dave Rodman.[31]

The official pronouncement didn't take place until 5:16 p.m. Eastern Standard Time from Halifax Medical Center. Mike Helton, who had been NASCAR President for only a little more than a year, was given the awful task of sharing the devastating news roughly an hour and forty-five minutes later.

Earnhardt's death completed a two-year string of tragedies that was reminiscent of the high-profile losses endured between 1964 and 1965, as well as the deaths that took place from 1992 to 1994. But unlike any of the others, this catastrophic loss would have the farthest-reaching impact on the sport's safety measures.

Certainly Adam Petty's death had made an immediate difference. For example, both the so-called kill switch and an anti-spill bladder in the fuel cells were mandated after his fatal crash in Loudon a year earlier.

But when Earnhardt died due to blunt force trauma to the head, NASCAR made one of its boldest moves yet by requiring that all drivers use the "head and neck support" (HANS) device, an apparatus that stops the head from whipping forward during the crash. Earnhardt himself, as well as other drivers like Mark Martin, had refused to use the device or anything similar to it due to its constrictive nature and the belief that it could cause more injuries than it might prevent.

When Superman Takes a Bullet

It might be easy to assume that MRO chaplain Dale Beaver was overwhelmed during the 2000 and 2001 seasons. After all, he was brand new to the scene and tasked with helping hundreds of people deal with unprecedented tragedy. But that was by no means the case.

"I'm completely convinced as to why God sent me to NASCAR for the time I was there," Beaver explains. "For some reason, I was the guy that had to be there during the time of the most trauma in NASCAR. From the time I got there until the time I left, I was dealing with a lot of funerals."[32]

Beaver was not only faced with the four driver deaths. He says that there were many crew members and their family members who had suffered losses due to car and motorcycle wrecks and even some instances of suicide. But naturally, it was Earnhardt's death that stirred up the greatest level of soul searching. As Schrader once told Beaver, "Everybody pays attention when Superman takes a bullet."

"Chapel attendance boomed for a while," Beaver says. "We had about a six-week window where people were really trying to get some closure and clarity about what this was all about and how they could deal with it."[33]

On a personal level, Beaver observed some drivers who had been marginally involved in ministry begin to increase their desire for spiritual growth. Bobby Labonte and Matt Kenseth, for instance, were among the Christian drivers who started taking more solid steps in their faith journey and becoming more comfortable talking about it publicly.

"I believe that when it's your day [to go], it's your day," Kenseth says. "God's more in control than we are. Obviously, you still take all the precautions and safety measures inside your car. When you go through a period like when Dale died and Adam died and Kenny Irwin and Tony Roper and those guys, it was a really tough time, and you can't help but think about it. You can't help think about what's going on, and that you could be next if you make a mistake."[34]

There were also some surprises.

"After Earnhardt died, I had conversations about faith with guys I never thought I would," Beaver says. "It paved the way for authenticity. Death always does that, especially when it's in a sport."[35]

Chapel service and other related activities eventually went back to business as usual, but before that happened, the events of the 2000 and 2001 seasons also impacted Raceway Ministries. Dr. Roger Marsh had been working with the organization since 1997 and was appointed the national director in 2001. After Earnhardt's death, NASCAR sped up its cooperation for expansion into most of the tracks where Raceway Ministries had yet to gain access. There was also an immediate need for help in dealing with unexpected reactions from the fans.

"I got a phone call from the guest services people at NASCAR," Marsh says. "They said, 'We've got people asking questions that we can't answer about death and heaven and eternity. Can your people help us out?' They had several things they wanted us to help them out with and I said yes to every one of them."[36]

And then came September 11, 2001. Having barely caught its

breath from its own tragedy seven months earlier, the racing community, along with the rest of the United States, was left staggering
after the terrorist attacks on the World Trade Center towers in
New York and the Pentagon in Arlington, Virginia. Raceway
Ministries was again called upon for help.

"The NASCAR fans thought it was Armageddon time, and
NASCAR again came to us and said, 'We don't have time to answer
all of these questions, and we don't know how,'" Marsh says.[37]

Over the next year or so, Raceway Ministries volunteers and
chaplains at NASCAR and other racing venues all across the
nation began to find themselves busily involved in conversations
with race fans and others about spiritual and eternal concerns.

Amid the emotional chaos, Dale Earnhardt Jr. was simply trying
to make sense of it all. Beaver was especially attuned to the young
driver's state of mind.

"His dad's death was an incredibly crushing moment for him,"
Beaver says. "He had finally gotten to the place where he was
going to have the relationship with his dad that he had longed for
his whole life in a context that earned his dad's respect. I can't
imagine what that felt like to this kid."[38]

Beaver watched Earnhardt Jr. as he explored the deeper questions of life and faith. It was an epic struggle between what he was
feeling inside and what the outside world was trying to sell him.

"Dale got to that crossroads that the Bible talks about," Beaver
says. "You've got to count the costs. If you take this road, you've
got Budweiser and whoever else whispering in your ear. And then
you've got someone like me whispering the gospel into the other
ear. That's heavy for anybody. But in that context of what Dale was
going through, I imagine it was overwhelming."[39]

Fortunately, Petty, Irwin, Roper, and Earnhardt Sr. did not die in
vain. Many safety measures were put into place thanks to the hard
lessons learned in each of those fatal on-track incidents. But as
Beaver and the MRO team would soon find out, life inside the race

car wasn't always the most dangerous place. For the Christian driver, it could sometimes be just as treacherous standing atop the lofty platforms that the sport so readily provided.

NOTES

1. Dr. Jerry Punch, interview with the author, October 8, 2011.
2. A restrictor plate is a device installed at the intake of the engine that limits its power. It slows down acceleration and reduces the top speeds to a level that is considered safer for superspeedways.
3. Bobby Allison, interview with the author, February 14, 2012.
4. Ibid.
5. "Clifford Allison Dies in Practice-Run Crash," *New York Times*, August 14, 1992.
6. Bobby Allison, interview with the author, February 14, 2012.
7. Larry McReynolds, interview with the author, October 2, 2010.
8. Ed Hinton, "Requiem For A Racing Man," *Sports Illustrated*, July 26, 1993.
9. Bobby Allison, interview with the author, February 14, 2012.
10. Larry McReynolds, interview with the author, October 2, 2010.
11. Bobby Allison, interview with the author, February 14, 2012.
12. Dale Beaver, interview with the author, August 21, 2012.
13. Ibid.
14. Ibid.
15. Bobby Allison, interview with the author, February 14, 2012.
16. Ibid.
17. Dale Beaver, interview with the author, August 21, 2012.
18. Ibid.
19. Jim McCoy, "Remembering Dale—The Rivalries," *Bump-Drafts*, December 28, 2008 (http://bump-drafts.com/2008/12/28/remembering-dale-the-rivalries/).
20. Dale Grubba, *Alan Kulwicki, NASCAR Champion: Against All Odds* (San Francisco: Badger Books, 2009), 281.
21. McCoy, "Remembering Dale—The Rivalries."
22. Darrell Waltrip, interview with the author, October 2, 2010.
23. Larry McReynolds, interview with the author, October 2, 2010.
24. Dale Beaver, interview with the author, August 21, 2012.
25. Darrell Waltrip, interview with the author, October 2, 2010.
26. Andy Petree, interview with the author, October 18, 2011.
27. Buz McKim, interview with the author, January 31, 2012.
28. Larry McReynolds, interview with the author, October 2, 2010.
29. Darrell Waltrip, interview with the author, October 2, 2010.
30. Ibid.
31. Dave Rodman, "Schrader Recalls a Friend and the Frantic Moments after

the Crash," NASCAR.com, February 18, 2011
(http://www.nascar.com/en_us/news-media/articles/2011/02/18/dearnhardt
-kschrader-remembers-10.html).

32. Dale Beaver, interview with the author, August 21, 2012.
33. Ibid.
34. Matt Kenseth, interview with the author, November 1, 2008.
35. Dale Beaver, interview with the author, August 21, 2012.
36. Dr. Roger Marsh, interview with the author, February 17, 2012.
37. Ibid.
38. Dale Beaver, interview with the author, August 21, 2012.
39. Ibid.

CHAPTER 6

The Problem with Pedestals

Even though the ministry surge was short-lived after Dale Earnhardt Sr.'s death at Daytona in 2001, the residual effects lingered throughout the garage. It soon became commonplace for star drivers such as Dale Jarrett, Mark Martin, David Green, Robert Pressley, Kyle Petty, and Bobby Labonte to share their faith through various Motor Racing Outreach (MRO) materials and Christian media outlets.

But in the immediate aftermath, there were some unforeseen developments that put ministry outlets like MRO in some precarious situations.

Unintended Consequences

Dale Earnhardt Jr. just wanted to get back in the car and drive. It was the best way he knew to deal with the painful reality that his father was gone. He also knew about his dad's friendship with Stevie Waltrip, and how she had been bringing him a Bible verse before every race. So Earnhardt Jr. decided to continue that tradition and have Waltrip bring him a sticky note too. She kept doing just that until the end of 2006 season. After that, she would send a fax or email to an MRO representative at the track, who would then write out the Scripture on a UPS label and hand it to Earnhardt Jr. before the race.

On February 26, 2002, the Cup series resumed at the North Carolina Speedway (now known as Rockingham) for the Dura Lube 400. Earnhardt Jr.'s hope for comfort behind the wheel was short-lived. On the race's first lap he lost control of his car and hit the wall between the third and fourth turns. On March 4, at the UAW-Daimler Chrysler 400 in Las Vegas, Earnhardt fared a little better but was somewhat disappointed with a twenty-third-place finish.

In the meantime, the Christian Broadcasting Network (CBN) had reached out to Dale Beaver about doing a feature on MRO for its popular television program *The 700 Club*. As part of the special, the producers wanted to interview some of the drivers to find out how MRO had influenced their lives. In particular, *The 700 Club* wanted to talk to Earnhardt Jr. about how his and Beaver's relationship had grown since the two had entered the sport around the same time.

Earnhardt Jr.'s media team was skeptical. They were afraid that the producers might take advantage of the situation and ask the grieving driver some questions that he wasn't ready to answer— questions about his religious beliefs and his father's death. But Beaver convinced them that everything would be all right.

When interviewer Scott Ross and the production crew arrived at Atlanta Motor Speedway, they set up shop in Earnhardt Jr.'s hauler. It was later revealed that *The 700 Club* had been granted the interview based on the conditions that Earnhardt Jr. would answer two questions about Beaver, and that he would not be asked anything about his father.[1]

Just twenty days after the tragedy in Daytona, this "exclusive" interview (as *The 700 Club* would later promote it) took an immediate turn for the worst as Ross veered from the agreed-upon topic. The young driver graciously answered his questions anyway, until publicist Jade Gurss cut the interview short. Gurss wrote about the incident in his book *In the Red*:

While Ross led another prayer, his producer stepped outside to grab a large backpack. When she unzipped the bag, it wasn't filled with videotapes or camera gear, but an assortment of Dale Jr. diecast cars, hats, and other merchandise for Junior to autograph. Dale Jr. politely signed, and they were gone.[2]

When the segment aired, Beaver was mentioned only once. The focus was supposed to be on MRO and the chaplaincy program, but instead it was all about the very thing that Earnhardt Jr. had not yet talked about publicly.

"Dale Jr. was very uncomfortable [during that interview]," Beaver recalls. "He gave genuine answers. I think he wanted to go [down that road]. I think he was desperate to talk about it. But at the same time, it was something he wasn't ready to talk about."[3]

And while Earnhardt Jr. fans and others within the NASCAR community seethed over what *The 700 Club* had perpetuated, Beaver took full responsibility.

"That was a mistake," he says. "It was the worst mistake that I ever made. Dale Jr. and Jade Gurss, those guys were forgiving to me on that, but that changed my relationship with Dale Jr. I wish I would have trusted the PR people that were warning me about what might happen. If I could go back in time, I would take that weekend back."[4]

Beaver remained as the Cup chaplain through the 2005 season, but when he sees the picture of him and Earnhardt Jr. hanging from the wall in his office in Evansville, Indiana, where Beaver now serves on staff at Christian Fellowship Church, he still has the kind of regret that often accompanies unintended consequences.

"Dale Jr. trusted me completely from the time he started in this sport," Beaver says. "If you were to go to him now and he'd be really honest with you as to what he thinks about me and the message that I walked among those people with, I think he'd probably give me some grace. But that [situation with *The 700 Club*] is something I'd really like to take back."5

Christian Trophies

Ever since the advent of the Christian professional athlete, varying levels of public expressions of faith have emerged from within each of those national platforms. For instance, Major League Baseball had groundbreaking athletes such as second baseman Bobby Richardson, who played for the New York Yankees during the 1950s and 1960s and consistently used his platform to share the gospel. The "faith movement" among National Football League players, on the other hand, was led by the likes of quarterback Roger Staubach, who starred for the Dallas Cowboys during the 1970s while actively supporting the Fellowship of Christian Athletes.

By 2001, NASCAR personalities had been navigating the choppy waters of faith for just over fifty years. Most drivers held their beliefs privately and stayed in the background but were very supportive of those on the frontlines of motorsports ministry. It was always understood that drivers such as Ned Jarrett, Bobby Allison, and Richard Petty held deeply religious beliefs. Darrell Waltrip and his close friends Lake Speed, Bobby Hillin Jr., and Phil Parsons also made an impact during the 1980s. But even then, there had not yet been an A-list star in his prime take the opportunity to use such an enormous platform for the express purpose of spreading the gospel message.

That all changed when a hotshot driver from California hit the scene. Jeff Gordon had been a dominant force in the United States Auto Club's midget car series from 1989 to 1992, but during that stretch he got his first shot at NASCAR when he debuted at the

Busch Series race at Rockingham on October 20, 1990. Gordon's career especially took off in 1991, when he was named Busch Series Rookie of the Year followed by a three-win season in 1992. His success there vaulted him into a Cup ride with Hendrick Motor Sports in the iconic DuPont-sponsored #24 car.

It was during that time when Gordon started attending chapel services at the track, thanks to his growing friendship with Bobby Hillin Jr. Gordon was also influenced by Darrell Waltrip and MRO chaplain Max Helton.

"Max was a big influence for me," Gordon told interviewer Dave Caldwell in 2001. "I admired him for a lot of different reasons. He never really was pushing people into it. He just very subtly would talk to me about God."[6]

After winning a qualifying race for the 1993 Daytona 500, Gordon's spiritual life took another turn when he met the reigning Miss Winston, Brooke Sealey, in Victory Lane. The two secretly dated until she gave up her crown at the end of the season, and they were married the following year in November. Helton performed the ceremony. Not long before the wedding, Gordon was baptized in his fiancée's home church in King, North Carolina.[7]

"[Religion] was a part of her life," Gordon said. "It was important to her, and she wanted it to be important to the person she was with. A lot of the [religious] questions that I felt I couldn't just ask of anybody, I felt I could ask her. I really became interested in it, and my belief just grew and grew and grew."[8]

Much as Stevie Waltrip had done for her husband, Darrell Waltrip, and Dale Earnhardt Sr., Sealey routinely taped a Scripture verse to Gordon's steering wheel. At a summer race during the 2001 season, for instance, she wrote 1 Corinthians 15:57, which says, "Thanks be to God, who gives us the victory," along with a personal note, "Be safe. I love you."[9]

By then, it seemed as though Gordon was fairly comfortable talking about his faith, albeit still in general terms. And even early on in his spiritual journey, the temptation for ministry leaders to cover the attention that such a high-profile Christian athlete might bring was too difficult to resist.

One of Gordon's first prominent speaking engagements came on June 22, 1996, when the reigning Cup champion made a surprise appearance at a Promise Keepers[10] event at Charlotte Motor Speedway in front of fifty thousand men.

"In a race, there is only one winner," he told the pumped-up audience. "But when you bring Christ into your life, you're all winners."[11]

When Beaver arrived on the scene to take the reins from Helton, he quickly realized that the two chaplains had one significant philosophical difference.

"I never had someone pass a leadership position off to me like Max did," Beaver says. "It was beautiful. That guy was a mentor to me in ways that very few men have been. I wouldn't trade my time walking with him for anything. But Max came from that school of thought that said once you become a believer, you give your testimony. That's just what you do. It was purely well-intentioned on Max's part. But the problem was that Max was also under pressure from the Christian community that wanted its hero and potential donors who were out there giving money to the ministry because you were making a difference in the lives of these drivers. They wanted to see the fruit of that. The fruit means you bring them to their event and let him share their testimony. These guys weren't ready to do that. It put them in a tough place."[12]

Billy Mauldin, who, like Beaver, joined the MRO staff full-time in 1999, also observed what was going on and can, in hindsight, clearly see some mistakes that were made along the way.

"Jeff was early in his racing career when he came to know Christ," he explains. "Because of his stardom, he should have honestly been left alone to grow in his faith a little bit longer before he was taken out to Promise Keepers and things like that. A lot of these guys haven't gone through a transformation yet. We as the church need to learn to hold off a little bit and not rush these guys out there as witnesses for Christ before they've had a chance to really know the Lord."[13]

Gordon's close friend Bobby Hillin Jr. was wary of the situation from the start. He knew that Gordon had a great heart, and that his desire to get closer to God was real. But he also knew that the effort to push young Christian drivers like Gordon into the public arena was a dangerous proposition.

"I was very judgmental about the way MRO, specifically Max, would mark off the checklist," Hillin says. "'So-and-so is a Christian now. Let's go promote him now.' I was very skeptical and very judgmental at the time. And now, I wish I hadn't been so skeptical and so judgmental, because maybe I could have helped some of those guys grow in their faith more. But because I was so high on my horse, I didn't do that."[14]

By the end of the 2001, Gordon was riding high. He had just won his fourth Cup championship in six years, and at that time he trailed only seven-time winners Richard Petty and Dale Earnhardt Sr. in the record books.[15]

But the next season would bring two significant changes. On the track, Gordon was gaining a new teammate. Jimmie Johnson had run three races for Hendrick Motor Sports in 2001, and now the #48 car was about to tackle his first season in the Cup series. Gordon would finish a respectable fourth in the standings that year, but many racing pundits wondered if Johnson's upstart team might have taken away from the #24 car's quest for a fifth title.

Nothing, however, would challenge Gordon more than the personal battle that was brewing away from the track. When the NASCAR community rolled into Darlington for the 2002 season's fifth race, it was greeted with the shocking news that Gordon's wife was filing for divorce. Over the next fifteen months the estranged couple was tabloid fodder and the target of disappointed Christians and disillusioned fans.

Long after the divorce settlement that was reached in June 2003, ministry leaders who had eagerly utilized Gordon in their evangelistic efforts were still left wondering where they had missed the mark.

"We take these guys that all of the sudden become Christians, and we start parading them out to be our new testimony to the importance of having a relationship with Christ," Mauldin admits. "Some of them haven't even developed their relationship with Christ. They've just come to know him. All of the sudden, they're being put out there, and I think we as the body of Christ have to take a little responsibility. We have a tendency to use these personalities as Christian trophies. 'Hey look! We got this one! Look what we caught!' But they haven't had a chance to walk with the Lord yet. They've just been introduced to him."

Mauldin adds, "When you think about the disciples, how many years did they walk with Jesus before they even really got it fully? Peter was still denying [Jesus] three years later. Yet we expect these guys who have just accepted Christ to start speaking at the Billy Graham Crusade. That's foolish on our part."[16]

Beaver likewise lamented the situation with Gordon. He had become close friends with the superstar driver over a relatively short period of time and recalls their last in-depth conversation. Ironically, it took place in Darlington, the same weekend when Gordon's divorce was made public.

"Now he's married again, and he's a dad," Beaver says. "I never imagined he would get married again much less have kids. Now he has this life that he seems to be loving. That's one thing I would pay for. I would pay for a weekend with Jeff again. I would ask him about the journey he's been on and what's happened since Darlington 2002."[17]

Hillin in particular struggled a great deal with Gordon's divorce. He now admits to having a very judgmental attitude toward his friend. But his own personal struggles nearly a decade later would open his eyes to the error of that mindset.

"I am divorced today," Hillin says. "God put me in my place. I realized that it doesn't matter how strong someone thinks they are in their faith. Anybody can fall. Anybody can have those situations where they make really bad decisions. Anybody can turn their back on God for a lot of reasons. I don't know where Jeff is right now today, but I can tell you from my perspective that I know unequivocally that I am far more effective for God today than I was as a married man ever. The manifestation of my Christian walk is so different today because I have a renewed sense of God's heart."[18]

Hillin has also come full circle in his belief that MRO and other Christian ministries like it do far more good than harm when dealing with high-profile Christian athletes.

"The bottom line is that Jeff knows who Jesus is, and there are a lot of guys like him that have been introduced to Christ," he says. "At the end of the day, they have a lot of opportunity to grow in their faith. It doesn't really matter how Jeff's situation was handled. All of those guys were introduced to God [through MRO], and they've been given the chance to grow in their own faith. They will [grow] in their own time."[19]

Quiet Faith

Though the NASCAR community did its best to shield Gordon from the onslaught, his personal troubles, predictably, induced a great deal of negative attention from the mainstream press. His public statements of faith leading up to his image-tainting divorce certainly didn't help matters.

Dale Beaver believes that what happened to Gordon also had a chilling effect on the rest of the garage, especially Christian drivers who might have been contemplating a more open public approach. It suddenly became too much of a risk to engage in public expressions of faith or to forge cozy associations with high-profile ministries.

"I think that was very true," Beaver says. "It hindered some of the faith that was potentially blooming in that sport."[20]

But there was still a large number of believers in the background and even some who were willing to lend their name to various ministry endeavors, such as a series of testimony cards and video interviews that had begun widely circulating to the fans. For those who chose to maintain a quiet faith, Beaver believes, it was often due to a much larger issue.

"They believed that their witness was cheapened because they were in competitive sports," he says. "They understood that people were always going to want to grade their [Christian] walk based on their win-loss record or their success on the track."[21]

That, of course, didn't mean that their faith was any less real. Joe Nemechek was one of those drivers who learned to rely heavily on his relationship with God when the uncertainties of car safety, financial stability, and spiritual unrest were commonplace during the century's first decade.

"If you don't have faith, you have nothing," he says. "Faith is number one. Believe me, I have my days when I start questioning stuff, but you take everything and put it in perspective. I've dealt with some tragedy in my life, like losing my brother [John, in 1997]. That was probably one of the hardest days when I've been tested. But you learn what things are important. You have to prioritize your life with your family, your friends, things you want to accomplish. You've got to get all that stuff in order, and having faith in these difficult times is very important."[22]

At the same time that veteran drivers such as Nemechek, Mark Martin, and Kyle Petty were setting the example behind the scenes, some younger drivers were following their lead and developing a quiet faith of their own.

Although Matt Kenseth had made his NASCAR debut in 1996, he didn't reach superstar status until he won his first Cup race at the 2000 Coca-Cola 600 in Charlotte, the same year he was named

Rookie of the Year. Kenseth's place among the sport's elite was further solidified in 2003, when he won the Cup championship.

Raised in a Methodist family, the Wisconsin native quickly gravitated toward racetrack ministry. He and his wife, Katie, received premarital counseling from former MRO leaders Ron and Jackie Pegram, and later they would spend time on the MRO board of directors. Former Cup chaplain Tim Griffin says that he always appreciated Kenseth's steady approach to life.

"Matt is a driver that has incredible composure," Griffin says. "Even though he's a straight talker, rarely is that mixed with inordinate emotion. He's just a very composed individual. He understands that this isn't the beginning and end of all things. So his reaction to certain on-track issues, he's going to handle like a professional because he's a very grounded individual."[23]

Kenseth has had a history of getting tangled up with other star drivers and then feeling their wrath in bizarre circumstances. In 2006 at Bristol, for instance, Jeff Gordon (with his helmet still on) angrily yelled at Kenseth in the pit area and then pushed him before being pulled away. A year later, Kenseth was doing a trackside television interview at Martinsville when Carl Edwards walked by and shoved him out of the camera. The two argued for a few moments about a recent on-track incident, and then Edwards infamously threw a fake punch before walking away.

Kenseth says that in those moments, even when he's not instigating trouble (which he rarely does), he tries to rely on his faith to handle those situations with integrity, but it doesn't always work out that way.

"I'm far from perfect," he confesses. "There's a lot of times you'll say something that you regret or do something that you regret and wish you wouldn't have said it or done it. But, if you try to take a moment and think about it and try to make good decisions and think about the consequences or how the other person might feel instead of just react, that's probably the best thing to do. In our business that's kind of hard to do because things happen too fast. But when you at least try to do that, things turn out better more times than not."[24]

Throughout his early career, second-generation driver David Reutimann did a reasonably good job staying above the fray. In many ways, Reutimann is the same shy, laid-back guy he was when he broke into the NASCAR ranks back in 2002. Like Kenseth, he has espoused a quiet but sincere faith in Christ.

"That was something I didn't know about David when I first met him," Darrell Waltrip says. "David is a solid guy. Once you're around him a little bit, then you realize what a great believer he is. David just keeps it to himself. That's kind of old school. But once you get to know him you realize that he's a solid guy—a good man."[25]

After spending five seasons working his way up the Nationwide Series ranks for owners such as Brian Pattie and Joe Nemechek, Reutimann finally caught on with fellow Kentuckian Michael Waltrip and his upstart Michael Waltrip Racing (MWR) team. Not long into his career at MWR, Reutimann decided to put a cross next to his name above the car window. It's a tradition that he has carried with him ever since, but not without some sobering realizations.

"It's been a struggle for me personally to have [the cross] up there," Reutimann says. "If you're going to have that on your car, you need to do things a certain way. People look at that and say, 'Listen to what he just said on the radio and he has a cross on his car?'"[26]

Reutimann fully acknowledges that such public expressions of faith are a sharp, double-edged sword. That was certainly the case in 2010 when an on-track feud with Kyle Busch resulted in an unfortunate incident at Kansas Motor Speedway on October 3. After feeling that Busch had been too aggressive earlier in the race, Reutimann later paid him back by slamming into Busch's #18 car and effectively ending not just Busch's chances to win the race, but his chances to challenge for the Cup title.

After climbing from his car, the cross above his window served as another reminder of just how precarious the life of a Christian athlete can be.

"The cross is there for me as a person because that's one of the last things I see when I get in the car so I can try to remind myself what that's all about," Reutimann says. "But sometimes it's a double-edged sword because I'm like, 'Man, I went out there and acted like that on the race track?' It's not always sending a very good message."[27]

While Reutimann was trying to find a balance between the two schools of thought on faith expression, a young driver from Unadilla, Georgia, was just trying to figure out what it was going to take to make it as a NASCAR driver. In 2004, just eighteen years old, David Ragan debuted in the Truck Series and the Nationwide Series. By 2007, he had earned the trust of car owner Jack Roush, who placed him in the #6 Cup car. As with Reutimann, racing fans wouldn't likely peg Ragan as an elite stock car racer away from the track.

"Most people might not even recognize David out of uniform," Griffin says. "He's such a humble guy that just walks around very quietly. He's a little like Mark Martin in that he's got that quiet, focused demeanor. He is not one of those guys that's going to clamor for the camera or look to run off at the mouth to be quoted somewhere. He's just not that kind of a guy."[28]

That was certainly the case with Ragan's public expressions of faith. Though not at all embarrassed to talk about his Southern Baptist upbringing, he wasn't necessarily looking to discuss it in detail unless asked.

"My grandparents and my mom and dad were great influences," Ragan explains. "I was very fortunate to have good family values and a lot of good people teaching me throughout the years. I grew up in a church that helped me have confidence in the Lord to work through tough situations. This world's a tough place to live in, and you have to have something to fall back on."[29]

In hindsight, Ragan turned out to be a precursor of what was to come. As a young driver with a rock solid faith in God, he would provide a bridge between the behind-the-scenes faithful living of the older generation and a new group of voices that were about to emerge. MRO had learned some hard lessons about the athlete-ministry dynamic and would be better prepared to handle the evangelistic boom that was just around the corner.

NOTES

1. Dale Beaver, interview with the author, August 21, 2012.
2. Jade Gurss, *In the Red: The 2001 Season with Dale Earnhardt Jr.* (Austin: Octane Press, 2012).
3. Dale Beaver, interview with the author, August 21, 2012.
4. Ibid.
5. Ibid.
6. Dave Caldwell, "A Talk with Jeff Gordon," BeliefNet, August 2001 (http://www.beliefnet.com/Faiths/Christianity/2001/08/A-Talk-With-Jeff-Gordon.aspx).
7. Dave Caldwell, "Godspeed," BeliefNet, August 2001 (http://www.beliefnet.com/Faiths/Christianity/2001/08/Godspeed.aspx).
8. Ibid.
9. Ibid.
10. Promise Keepers is a Christian men's organization founded in 1990 by Bill McCartney, who at that time was head coach of the University of Colorado football team. The organization was especially known throughout the 1990s and early 2000s for hosting large gatherings of men in stadiums and large arenas across the United States.
11. Jeff Gordon, testimony given at Promise Keepers rally, Charlotte Motor Speedway, June 22, 1996.
12. Dale Beaver, interview with the author, August 21, 2012.
13. Billy Mauldin, interview with the author, December 5, 2011.
14. Bobby Hillin Jr., interview with the author, February 10, 2012.
15. Jeff Gordon has since been surpassed by Hendrick Motor Sports teammate Jimmie Johnson, who won his fifth Cup championship in 2010.
16. Billy Mauldin, interview with the author, December 5, 2011.
17. Dale Beaver, interview with the author, August 21, 2012.
18. Bobby Hillin Jr., interview with the author, February 10, 2012.

19. Ibid.
20. Dale Beaver, interview with the author, August 21, 2012.
21. Ibid.
22. Joe Nemechek, interview with the author, October 7, 2011.
23. Tim Griffin, interview with the author, November 5, 2008.
24. Matt Kenseth, interview with the author, November 1, 2008.
25. Darrell Waltrip, interview with the author, October 2, 2010.
26. David Reutimann, interview with the author, October 8, 2011.
27. Ibid.
28. Tim Griffin, interview with the author, November 5, 2008.
29. David Ragan, interview with the author, October 31, 2008.

CHAPTER 7

The Trevor Bayne Effect

It was a surreal moment when Trevor Bayne hoisted the massive Daytona 500 trophy on February 20, 2011. A few hours earlier, the idea of the barely twenty-year-old winning "The Great American Race" would have been nothing more than a NASCAR fantasy. Who wouldn't love to see the young man take the checkered flag driving in the storied #21 Wood Brothers Ford? So many amazing storylines could be told.

For instance, it was just Bayne's second Sprint Cup start. He had lost his Nationwide ride with Michael Waltrip Racing four months earlier before getting picked up by Roush Fenway Racing and placed in what was essentially a nonsponsored car. Bayne would also be the youngest Daytona 500 winner, ironically supplanting his idol, Jeff Gordon, who was twenty-five when he won the race in 1997. Bayne's victory would no doubt be argued as the biggest upset in the race's history, and of course, it would mark the long-overdue return to Victory Lane for the Wood Brothers, who had last won in Daytona with David Pearson back in 1976—fifteen years before Bayne was born.

But here the infectiously smiling Knoxville native stood, confetti falling around him, shocked fans cheering an unlikely historic hero, the media basking in its opportunity to report one of the great recent moments in all of sports. As Bayne climbed from his car, he conspicuously pointed his right index to the sky followed by a brief glance heavenward. And then, in his first response to Fox Sports reporter Krista Voda, he made a statement that would set the tone for the next nine months.

"We said a prayer before [the race], and you know we pray a lot," Bayne said. "We expect a lot of things, but this just shows how powerful God is."[1]

Before then, only those in the garage, the most ardent fans, and a handful of Christian publications had caught wind of Bayne's penchant for the public expression of faith. But now, it was front and center for millions of television viewers to see.

A New Kind of Boy's Club

For the better part of the previous decade there had seemed to be a lull of activity as far as outspoken high-profile drivers were concerned. Darrell Waltrip had been camped in the broadcast booth since his retirement in 2000, and Dale Jarrett had left the ranks in 2008 and by then was not nearly as vocal as he had been while racing for Joe Gibbs in the mid-1990s. Another noted believer, Kyle Petty, was unceremoniously ousted from his #45 car at Petty Enterprises in 2006.

There certainly were others who espoused a strong Christian faith, but many of them, such as Matt Kenseth, Mark Martin, David Ragan, and Bobby Labonte, were more soft-spoken in their approach. Several drivers, including Ryan Newman, Greg Biffle, and Jimmie Johnson, even provided financial and vocal support for Motor Racing Outreach (MRO), but they were by no means prepared to profess openly a detailed commitment to any specific spiritual belief system.

At the Nationwide Series level, however, there were inklings of a change in 2007 when a young driver, Brad Coleman, turned his successful Automobile Racing Club of America career into an opportunity with Joe Gibbs Racing. In 2008 Michael McDowell became a consistently present figure driving for Michael Waltrip Racing at the Sprint Cup level and later for various Nationwide and Sprint Cup teams. That same season, Sam Hornish made the full-time leap from IndyCar to Sprint Cup, racing in the #77 car for Roger Penske. Justin Allgaier was another up-and-coming Christian driver who, like Hornish, caught his big break with Penske driving the #12 Nationwide Series car late in 2008 and throughout the next two seasons. All four drivers represented a shift from the brash "young gun" mentality that had been exemplified in drivers such as Kyle Busch, Denny Hamlin, and Kasey Kahne.

As the 2010 season approached, two new faces were ready to join NASCAR's growing youth movement. A year earlier, Trevor Bayne had raced a part-time schedule in Michael Waltrip Racing's #99 car, while Ricky Stenhouse Jr. had been given a golden opportunity spelling Sprint Cup drivers in the #6 Roush Fenway car.

But something else took place at the beginning of the 2010 schedule that would prove especially significant. At the time, Lonnie Clouse was MRO's lead chaplain for the Nationwide Series. Seeing an influx of young Christian talent emerging upon the scene, Clouse created a Bible study group to help them deal with the challenging NASCAR lifestyle. Early on, Allgaier, Bayne, McDowell, and Stenhouse were regular participants. Other Christians on the circuit, such as Eric McClure, attended the Saturday morning meeting when their busy schedules allowed.

"The Bible study group wasn't anything new to our ministry," Clouse says. "It was something that a previous chaplain named Eddie Robinson had done years ago before he became a missionary. When he left, the Bible study died off for quite a few years. I recognized that we had a great nucleus of young guys, and we needed to get it up and running. I worked on it for about six months, and it was slow getting it going, but once I built more relationships with them and they got to spend more time with each other, it just took off. Before we knew it, we were meeting every week."[2]

Clouse started out by taking the group through a popular Christian book called *Crazy Love* by best-selling author and national speaker Francis Chan. From there, Clouse could see bonds forming between the young men. They began keeping one another accountable and spending more time together away from the track.

"From there, we were looking for platforms that would allow them to share their faith," Clouse adds. "We took them out to the fans and did whatever we could through Raceway Ministries. We also looked at local church opportunities, and then we did driver testimony cards and put them on our website. It humbles me to see how much is being accomplished for the kingdom through these young guys and the platform that God has given them."[3]

That first year was trying for some of the drivers involved, including Stenhouse, who dealt with early season car troubles and untimely wrecks. In hindsight, he acknowledges that it was the fellowship of the weekly Bible study that kept his head on straight and allowed him to bounce back and claim Nationwide Series Rookie of the Year honors.

"We struggled a lot that year," Stenhouse says. "But our small group kept building me up and not letting me get too hard on myself. I really relied on God and prayer and asked him to help me get through it. Of course, you had your friends to lean on too. Then after that we had a really good year. It turned out to be an awesome year."[4]

On the other hand, Bayne was having a great year and enjoying his spot in the top ten of the Nationwide Series standings when Michael Waltrip released him from the #99 car. Not knowing what would happen next, Bayne was quickly picked up by Roush Fenway Racing and placed in the mostly unsponsored #16 car for the remainder of the season.

Allgaier, however, ended up having the most successful season of those in the committed group of young Christians. He won his first career race at the Scotts Turf Builder 300 in Bristol and finished fourth in the final points standings. His year, however, wasn't devoid of unfortunate incidents. At the Federated Auto Parts 300 in Nashville, Allgaier, who was in sixth place at the time, made an aggressive move to pass Bayne. The hard contact cut Bayne's left rear tire and caused a spinout and nasty crash into the outside wall. When Bayne emerged from the car, he was clearly unhappy with Allgaier, although his remarks on the television broadcast were muted in comparison.

Asked about the incident four months later, Bayne laughed about his anger at the time and submitted that those tests to the small group would always be short-lived.

"We were in a Bible study earlier that morning," he smiled. "Growing up in the sport, I've been able to separate what happens on the track with what happens away from the track. That track is totally different. I'm not the same person when I put that helmet on. It's not Trevor Bayne. It's not Justin Allgaier. It's not Ricky Stenhouse. There's a race car, and I want to beat it. That helps with the pressure. It's just another car. If they crash me, I get upset, but I don't bring it off the track."[5]

Stepping Up to the Plate

Late in the 2010 season Lonnie Clouse stepped down from his post with MRO to join Back2Back Ministries, an organization that serves the needs of orphans in Mexico, Nigeria, India, and Haiti. That offseason, Bayne traveled to Monterrey, Mexico, for his first mission trip where Clouse was stationed at an orphanage. After returning to the United States in preparation for the 2011 season, Bayne continued to stay in touch with Clouse and continually sought out his mentor's spiritual advice.

"We'd been talking and emailing back forth and before the Daytona 500, and [Trevor] asked me to pray for him," Clouse recalls. "He was about to jump into a Cup ride, and he wanted to be the witness that God had called him to be through the highs and lows of the sport. He meant it very genuinely. It was almost prophetic when he talked to me that day."[6]

When Bayne won the Daytona 500, a media firestorm quickly ensued. He made appearances with David Letterman, Jay Leno, and Ellen DeGeneres, among other high-profile TV stops. His Bible study buddies vicariously enjoyed the experience. "He started pumping all of us up in the small group," Stenhouse Jr. recalls. "We were loving it."[7]

Clouse enjoyed Bayne's victory from south of the border and couldn't help think of some of the Bible study group's conversations the previous year.

"We had been talking about what Jesus said in Matthew 22, 'Love the Lord your God with all your heart,' and 'love your neighbor as yourself,'" he reminisces. "It blew my mind that Trevor was able to articulate those two things in the short period of time that he had on national television right after the race. He was able to share those things that we had studied in Bible study and those things that we had been working on. With all the pressure and all the cameras and everything going on, it was incredible to see how he handled that situation."[8]

Later that evening, Bayne called Clouse from the media center. The young driver who had just shocked the racing world was clearly moved by the life-changing event.

"Trevor broke down on the phone a little bit," Clouse says. "He said, 'Man, what just happened?' And I said, 'Remember how we talked about the highs and lows, buddy? You're at a high. What are you going to do with it?' So he just seized the day and went for it. He knew he didn't have the talent or the car. He knew he did not have what it took to win that race. He knew that it was the sovereignty of God that allowed him to be the winner of that race. He was going to make the most of it and do whatever he could to honor and glorify the Lord through it. From then on, in all of his interviews and in everything he did and said, he was a bright and shining light."9

But during the Sprint Cup's Samsung Mobile 500 on April 9 in Fort Worth, Bayne complained of numbness in his arm, and the morning after the Aaron's 499 in Talladega, he woke up with a severe case of double vision. Over the next five weeks, Bayne was put out of commission while doctors did their best to diagnose the culprit. The following January, it was revealed that Bayne had contracted Lyme disease after he was bitten by an infected tick.10

"What's kind of ironic to me is that Trevor went from winning the Daytona 500 to being laid up in the hospital and not knowing if he was going to get back behind the wheel of a race car or not," Allgaier says.11

"When Trevor got sick, it was like, 'Dangit!'" adds Stenhouse Jr. "That's not what we wanted. That's not what we needed. But if anybody could get through it, we knew Trevor could. We knew that he would be the strongest out of any of us to be able to go through that. We were there for him when he won the Daytona 500, and we were there for him when he wasn't racing."12

In the meantime, both Allgaier and Stenhouse Jr. found themselves in the middle of a heated Nationwide Series championship chase. Stenhouse Jr. ultimately won the title, with Allgaier finishing third. Along the way, Stenhouse Jr. won his first race at the John Deere Dealers 250 in Iowa, while Allgaier added a second race victory to his résumé at the STP 300 in Chicago.

Upon his return to the track five weeks later, Bayne struggled with the #16 car for a good portion of the season but eventually saw his results improve. He joined his friends in the win column by taking the checkered flag on November 6 at the O'Reilly Auto Parts Challenge in Fort Worth, and he finished eleventh in the points despite missing five races. One of the more powerful moments from the season came three weeks earlier, on October 15, when Bayne gave the pre-race invocation at the Sprint Cup's Bank of America 500 in Charlotte.

Bayne and his friends were afforded those kinds of opportunities in much greater volume since the beginning of the 2011 season. McDowell has been a regular speaker at ministry events away from the track, and even Stenhouse Jr., who is less outgoing than his good friend Bayne, has done some public speaking.

"[At the 2010 race in Talladega], I got up and talked about the power of prayer," Stenhouse Jr. says. "But Trevor is definitely a lot better at it than I am. I think that's just where he is in his walk with the Lord. We're a little different. Everybody can always grow, but Trevor is definitely the better speaker between the two of us, especially when it comes to stuff like that. But I have done it once. It's funny, I don't really get nervous about anything but I was definitely nervous doing that."[13]

In the process, this young group of drivers has caught the attention of Christian members of the media and some old-school racing legends alike. ESPN broadcaster and former crew chief Andy Petree says that Bayne is "such a role model for these other guys coming along."[14]

Fellow ESPN reporter Dr. Jerry Punch refers to the group as "a breath of fresh air."[15] Darrell Waltrip is especially encouraged by their youthful exuberance.

"It's exciting to me because these are young men," Waltrip says. "I didn't think about [spiritual things] until I was pretty far down the road in my career. I didn't think about giving the Lord any glory at all. It's exciting to me when I hear young men in this sport that give the Lord the credit for their success."[16]

Legendary driver Morgan Shepherd can always be spotted on the front row at the weekly Nationwide Series chapel service with Bayne, Allgaier, and Blake Koch, among others, sitting close behind.

"It is so encouraging to see in this day and time, with what goes on in the world, that you've got Trevor Bayne and Ricky Stenhouse and all the guys that truly love the Lord," Shepherd says. "Trevor Bayne, he is something else. That young man carries his Bible to the track. He stands up for what he believes in. That really impresses me that we've got a young group in our sport that's not afraid to speak out. They go out and walk the walk and talk the talk."[17]

Perhaps the most telling way the group walked that proverbial walk happened during the extreme highs and lows that the 2011 season presented them individually and collectively. Allgaier concurs that what Bayne went through was a rallying point for the others to be prepared for anything.

"Absolutely," he says. "We all shared in Trevor's win a little bit and Ricky's championship. But one thing that's really good about our deal is that we're always happy for each other when we're doing well, and we try to help each other when we're not doing well. That says a lot about our small group, because no matter how you want to put it, we're all selfish in certain ways, and we all want things that we can't have. Our group was definitely connected well, and it helped all of us."[18]

Full Speed Ahead

By the end of Bayne's crazy year, another high-profile athlete had turned the sports world on its head. Tim Tebow, then quarterback for the Denver Broncos and later traded to the New York Jets, became a lightning rod for the debate about the place of faith within the sports world. Bayne didn't have the same polarizing effect on NASCAR fans as Tebow did on NFL fans, but he has experienced some negative feedback on occasion.

"You get opposite ends," Bayne says. "I've never wanted to be that guy that stands on the middle ground. In a sense, you get the

Kyle Busch reaction. You get the people that love you, and you get the people that don't like you at all."[19]

In one instance, a Twitter follower responded to Bayne's overt expressions of faith: "Yeah, it's easy to thank God when things are good. What about when things are bad?"

"As soon as I got sick, I remembered that," Bayne says. "And I thought, 'This might be a chance to reach that one guy,' because [God is] still God. He's still the same. Even at Phoenix, the week after Daytona, I wrecked during practice and I tweeted, 'Well, He's still the same.' I don't know if that guy saw it or not, but you've just got to be consistent."[20]

Dr. Jerry Punch, who has publicly stated his support for Bayne and other Christian drivers, does offer some advice for outspoken believers who might be in for a rude awakening when it comes to mixing faith and their professional career.

"When you get in Victory Lane and someone says, 'I want to thank my Lord Jesus Christ,' people cringe," Punch says. "Even drivers that want to walk that walk sometimes feel a little concerned. Because what happens is—and they've been told this by their representatives—when you go that route, people turn off. So when you bring your sponsor up next, then you've already lost them. It's better to show your faith and live your faith than it is to shout it. Sometimes being a role model is better than preaching it from the mountaintop."[21]

While Bayne and his cohorts may understand Dr. Punch's words of wisdom, they don't seem terribly concerned about any negative consequences that might come their way.

"You know, before this ever happened, I had a meeting with some of the people that are running my business stuff, running my finances and everything," Bayne says. "We sat down and talked about the goal of Trevor Bayne as a company, as a person, as anything. I told them, the goal, this is going to sound weird, but it's not to be the best race car driver, the most marketable, the most popular, but it's to build a platform and let God use us on the platform that he's building. I just want to stand on the platform he's putting under me. That's our goal."[22]

Earlier in the year, Stephen Keller had replaced Clouse as the Nationwide Series chaplain and leader of the Bible study group. At that time, about four or five drivers were attending. Thanks to those young men's efforts, the meetings have seen anywhere from eight to thirteen people attending.

"There's enough kid left in these guys that they're willing to live their faith," Keller says. "They don't want to sit on a pew and grow old in a church. They want to do something. A few times I've challenged them and told them that belief isn't just something in your head, it's something you do. So these guys took that, and a bunch of them started to go to Wal-Mart before races and buy a bunch of toiletries and food items. They'd take those things and some Bibles and find homeless people and pass the stuff out—and in dangerous areas. It was incredible. They just go out and do things like that."

Keller adds, "We've also talked about worship as a lifestyle. So they took it literally, and about five of them got together with two guitars and a djembe, and they just went to a spot in downtown Davidson [North Carolina] and decided to do worship songs right outside Starbucks. This is group of kids that wants to influence others. They want to make a difference."[23]

Keller has since turned the Nationwide chaplain reins over to former Richard Childress crew member Nick Terry in an effort to focus solely on the Sprint Cup series. So perhaps that's why he's especially excited to see what might happen with these young drivers as their individual careers advance and take them to the next level. Even if, as he predicts, four or five of them make it to the Cup circuit, it will spark evangelistic opportunities not seen since MRO was founded back in 1988.

"It's going to be pretty tremendous when they get [to the Cup level]," Keller says. "If you have five strong Christians entering

Sprint Cup, it begins to tip the odds a little bit. I just get excited about the possibilities a few years down the line."[24]

In a strange twist, Bayne entered the 2012 season without full sponsorship for his #16 Nationwide Series team. He ended up splitting time between his Roush Fenway ride and the #21 Wood Brothers Sprint Cup car. It provided yet another test of faith for this young man, who is convinced that, no matter what happens, he will make sure to use the notoriety of his Daytona 500 victory and any future triumphs for the purpose of telling others about Jesus.

Things turned around for Bayne that same year as it was announced that he would drive fulltime for Roush Fenway during the 2013 season, due to his friend Ricky Stenhouse's promotion to the Cup series, where he was slated to replace Matt Kenseth (who was departing for Joe Gibbs Racing) in the #17 car. And as both drivers will openly attest, any opportunities that they receive have a far greater purpose than simply winning races.

"This is such a great platform," Bayne says. "There aren't many times you can be on ESPN giving God glory. That's what drives me to be successful here. [God's] provided this, so let's make the best of it. That's why I think he'll continue to keep me here, because it *is* a platform, and we have the talent and the ability. Better use it."[25]

NOTES

1. Trevor Bayne, interview by Krista Voda, *Daytona 500*, Fox Sports, February 20, 2011.
2. Lonnie Clouse, interview with the author, August 21, 2012.
3. Ibid.
4. Ricky Stenhouse Jr., interview with the author, October 7, 2011.
5. Trevor Bayne, interview with the author, October 1, 2010.
6. Lonnie Clouse, interview with the author, August 21, 2012.
7. Ricky Stenhouse Jr., interview with the author, October 7, 2011.
8. Lonnie Clouse, interview with the author, August 21, 2012.
9. Ibid.
10. "Bayne Reveals Illness Diagnosis," Crash.net, January 25, 2012 (http://www.crash.net/nascar/news/176224/1/bayne_reveals_illness_diagnosis.html).

11. Justin Allgaier, interview with the author, January 17, 2012.
12. Ricky Stenhouse Jr., interview with the author, October 7, 2011.
13. Ibid.
14. Andy Petree, interview with the author, October 18, 2011.
15. Dr. Jerry Punch, interview with the author, October 8, 2011.
16. Darrell Waltrip, interview with the author, October 2, 2010.
17. Morgan Shepherd, interview with the author, October 5, 2011.
18. Justin Allgaier, interview with the author, January 17, 2012.
19. Trevor Bayne, interview with the author, October 7, 2011.
20. Ibid.
21. Dr. Jerry Punch, interview with the author, October 8, 2011.
22. Trevor Bayne, response to question by the author during press conference call, February 22, 2011.
23. Stephen Keller, interview with the author, October 9, 2011.
24. Ibid.
25. Trevor Bayne, interview with the author, October 1, 2010.

CHAPTER 8

Weekend Warriors

It has long been argued that NASCAR is made unique by its fan base, but those who have been around the sport for very long understand that one of stock car racing's most unique aspects lies within the participants themselves.

That group extends well beyond the drivers and their crews and encompasses roughly 3,200 people who travel every week from one city to the next for thirty-six races every year. It includes executives, officials, publicists, sponsors, media, vendors, inspectors, and, of course, the ministry representatives who serve them all.

"You could use the word *family*, but that might come across overly mushy," Motor Racing Outreach (MRO) president Billy Mauldin says. "If I picked a different word, I would describe it as a tribe. There's a lot of loyalty and faithfulness within a tribe. You live together. You have a sense of community. Within that there are elements of family, but there's also squabbling and competition. It's a very competitive environment. People aren't afraid to step on one another's toes. But at the same time, when you talk about a tribe, if anyone from the outside comes in to threaten the tribe, they all rally around each other, and that's when it begins to look like family. The same is true for a traumatic situation like a death within the community. You see this tribe surround itself and support each other."[1]

Stephen Keller doesn't claim to be an expert on the inner workings of other sports organizations, but since joining MRO in June 2010, the Cup chaplain has gotten a pretty good idea of what else makes NASCAR, specifically its competitors, so distinctive.

"These guys seem more connected," Keller says. "They're all on different race teams, but there's camaraderie throughout the garage. Even when they trade words or mix it up verbally or with their cars on the track, it's a real tight-knit family. These guys really protect each other. They really care about each other. I've seen some of the most sworn enemies hanging out together. They also share more here. They share more resources, information, and they share a track every weekend. They even practice at the same places."[2]

And just like everywhere else, there are Christians rubbing shoulders with nonbelievers in close quarters weekend after weekend. Ricky Stenhouse Jr. agrees that NASCAR is essentially a microcosm of the real world, and that's why ministry at the track is so vital.

"The NASCAR drivers are a very diverse group of people," he says. "It's just a traveling city. You've got the same guys every week. You've got people that work in their trailers. You've got people that work in the media center. It's just a normal life for us all living on the road."[3]

Weekend Warriors

The numbers fluctuate from year to year, but in 2012, for instance, about fifty thousand campers descended upon Texas Motor Speedway for the AAA Texas 500. The scene is similar at other tracks throughout the year, such as Talladega, Atlanta, Daytona, Bristol, Sonoma, and Pocono.

But before the first fan arrives in a personal motor home (usually at noon on Thursday) or the first hauler pulls into the infield (usually at 6:00 a.m. on Thursday for Nationwide Series races), something else significant takes place. By Wednesday evening, members of the MRO ministry team arrive at the track, find the organization's assigned parking area inside the drivers' lot, and start preparing for the next four days of activity. On Thursday morning the real work begins.

Melanie Self has been on the MRO staff since 1998, and she has been serving as the full-time women's and children's ministry coordinator since 2001. She and her husband, Monty, a retired Air Force veteran now acting as MRO's director of operations, are greatly responsible for setting up the community center program, which hosts, among other things, Bible studies, family events, childcare, and the Bible kids' club, all of which are services provided to the drivers and their teams. The goal is to be open by 5:00 p.m. on Thursday for the families to utilize. But before that can happen, groceries must be purchased, toys must be sanitized and put in their places, and workers must be in position as people begin to check in and see what's been planned for that weekend.

"Imagine with me that this is your neighborhood," Self says. "We're just a mobile neighborhood. There are a hundred houses. There is a community center where you can host events or whatever your community needs. We provide toys and games. We plan activities based on seasonal events. It's not different than what a church would do. For a lack of a better word, I think the early folks who wanted a presence in the NASCAR neighborhood would refer to it as a steeple. So the community center ends up being that point of reference for people."[4]

On Friday, while practice sessions and qualifying laps are underway, the community center is in full swing with activities for kids and spouses. In the garage area chaplains meander to see who might need a shoulder to lean on or something simple like a smile or an encouraging word. In the evening, after things settle down, there might be a seasonal event, such as a fall festival, or something for holidays such as Easter, Mother's Day, or Father's Day.

On Saturday morning a group of young drivers routinely gathers for a weekly Bible study. At some point in the weekend, some of the wives will also assemble as Melanie Self leads them in their own time with the Scriptures. During that day's race, children at the track will take part in Bible club activities.

"They can make a mess of our place and go home, and we'll clean it up," Self says. "That steeple is hugely important so people can know that there's a place nearby. When there is something up, it will be one of the first places that they come. It takes my breath away every time. They may not have a kid or ever come to chapel. But it doesn't matter."5

Self also describes MRO as "a footprint in the neighborhood."6 Joe Nemechek has seen that footprint grow, shrink back, and grow again since his NASCAR career started back in 1990.

"When we first started having kids, it seemed like everybody around was having kids," he says. "All the sudden, MRO got bigger and bigger, and then there was a gap there where there weren't a lot of kids, so the organization shrunk back. Now the younger families are having more children, and it's growing a little bit more. It's neat to look back and see how it started with two or three couples getting together and how it's grown. They've touched so many different people's lives. It's just amazing."7

Mark Martin is another veteran driver who has greatly benefited from MRO's presence at the track. Not only did his son Matt grow up in the Bible club, but Martin also relied on the ministry to help him shore up the gaps in his faith walk.

"As you know, you use it [your faith] or lose it," he says. "Through all the years of my career, when I've had to work on my own race cars and drive up and down the road in the haulers, that was sort of a time period when you're sort of losing it because you weren't able to use it. I always have to thank Max Helton and everyone from MRO who enabled me to grow and to practice and surround myself with other people that had a hunger (to grow in their faith) as well. It's an incredible organization that has meant so much to me and my family."[8]

Because guys such as Nemechek and Martin have supported MRO in the past, younger drivers such as Michael McDowell can enjoy the accountability that comes from having chaplains hanging around their workplace.

"What MRO does at the racetrack is great," he says. "If you think about it, our season is from Valentine's Day to Thanksgiving. There's only one week off between all that. We race on Saturday, and we race on Sunday. Church for us is here at the racetrack. Our community is here at the racetrack. It's so important to have them here to pray with you when you need prayer and to rejoice with you when you need to rejoice. We have that church body here at the racetrack, and it's been awesome for us."[9]

Ricky Stenhouse Jr. can't imagine what it would be like if there were no ministry at the track.

"It would be tough," he says. "It's cool to have those guys there whenever you need them. They don't just preach us the Word. They're there for anything we need. They're there every weekend, and they don't get paid that much to do it. I think it's cool that they put that much time into it."[10]

How Great Thou Art

Between chapel services, community center events, Bible studies, and good old-fashioned personal interaction, Keller estimates that MRO impacts at least two thousand people each race weekend. Even though there are church-related ministry activities that take place, he believes that it's better to view what the organization does in different light.

"NASCAR is a mission field," Keller explains. "That separates this work from traditional church ministry. We're more like a parachurch ministry. Seeing it like a mission field makes a big difference.

The people in the NASCAR community are highly relational. If someone were to try to approach them with a church program or ministry out of a box, you wouldn't get five seconds with them. But it's through relationships, and a lot of times we're ministering out of crisis. These guys are on the road for so long. They get lonely. Someone might get sick back home. We're going to share tragedies and hardships out here. When you step in the midst of that, it's amazing how much ministry happens."[11]

During the 2011 season, for instance, Keller was able to make a difference in the life of one man from the NASCAR community who was going through some difficult personal issues. His wife had left him early in the season, and his anger was "just off the chart."

"But week after week, I would share the little bit I could with him about marriage, forgiveness—anything positive and encouraging that I could," Keller says. "Over time, that led to a little bit of prayer. It progressed to him asking for some material that he could read that could help him look at himself. Then he started to get involved in chapel. And toward the end of the year, that man accepted Christ. It makes you realize that if you take out any one of those conversations, that doesn't happen. It energized me. I was so excited about everything that's going on out here because of something tremendous that happened with this man."[12]

Sometimes it's not even about building relationships. Sometimes it's just about being present. On October 2, 2010, at Kansas Speedway, Keller was leading the Nationwide Series chapel service in the press conference room. His special guest was a local worship leader, Kenny Carter, who opened service with a congregational chorus. Later in the service Carter returned to lead drivers Morgan Shepherd, Ricky Stenhouse Jr., Justin Allgaier, and Trevor Bayne, among others, in an acoustic rendition of the classic hymn "How Great Thou Art."

But the song's greatest impact was made on someone who was not even in the room. A female reporter for a racing news website could hear the familiar tune playing from an adjacent press workroom. She broke away from what she was doing and made her way to the back row of the makeshift chapel. Afterward, she approached Carter and told him that she hadn't been to church in several weeks. When she heard "How Great Thou Art," she was prompted to take some time to reflect on her spiritual well-being.

The woman's story, while unusual and not the norm for how MRO impacts those in the NASCAR community, is still a reflection of just how powerful on-site ministry can be.

"It's surprising how many times people will come to Christ out here," Keller says. "That's a real shocker. That year alone, we probably had ten, fifteen people go from a place of not wanting to have anything to do with the church or God, and now they're in chapel every week. We're praying with them. They're just in this beautiful place of [spiritual] transformation."[13]

The Outer Circle

Depending on the venue, anywhere from an estimated 60,000 to 150,000 fans gather in the stands and the infield camping areas to watch any one of NASCAR's thirty-six races each year. Even though attendance figures steadily dropped during the economic downturn between 2008 and 2013, NASCAR has remained one of the most popular professional sports in the United States, second only to the National Football League.

When Frank Stark first saw the need for ministry to racing enthusiasts at Daytona International Speedway in 1976, the fan base was already experiencing incredible turnouts. And even though so much evangelistic effort, such as that of the MRO, is geared toward the high-profile individuals and those within NASCAR's inner circle, the fan-focused efforts of Raceway Ministries have continued to make sure that the spiritual needs of those in the "outer circle" are also addressed.

Like the more internally focused MRO, Raceway Ministries'
weekend starts before the fans are allowed to begin parking their
motor homes on the campgrounds outside of the track or on the
infield camping areas. At a typical four-day event, the local volunteers are set up and ready to serve by noon on Thursday.

Different tracks are configured differently, and different access
is available to racing ministries. For instance, at Daytona races,
Raceway Ministries sets up at the two available community center locations—one in the camping area and one in the infield. In
contrast, at Talladega, Raceway Ministries is permitted to have
tents in nine campground areas and is allowed to set up community centers under the walkway by the main gate and in the
infield. And then there are places such as Texas Motor
Speedway, where Raceway Ministries can set up tents and a
community center in the camping areas and chaplains have
access to the infield, but they are not allowed to set up a community center there. At a smaller track like Bristol there are ministry centers in all the campgrounds areas and an information
booth under the concourse of the grandstand, along with twenty to thirty chaplains stationed under the concourse and up in
the seats and in the infield.

"It always depends on the raceway," former Raceway Ministries
executive director Dr. Roger Marsh says. "My job was to do the
best I could to build healthy relationships with all the people
involved so we could create as much ministry opportunity as possible without being a burden to the raceway and without being a
problem. Raceway Ministries is not there to hit people over the
heads with Bibles. We're not there to harass people. We're there to
serve and share Christ whenever we have the opportunity to step
into [the fans'] lives."[14]

Raceway Ministries' service to the fans usually consists of
pancake breakfasts, horseshoe tournaments, counseling, and
chapel services that are also open to vendors and other track

workers. The volunteers provide golf cart rides for people who need assistance, and they stay in communication with guest services to respond if there's an injured fan, if someone needs to be notified of a death, or if a patron needs accompaniment for a hospital visit.

Children are another priority throughout the weekend. Raceway Ministries hosts puppet shows, pinewood derby races, and arts and crafts projects. More than anything, the tents are staffed twenty-four hours a day with a hot pot of coffee ready for anyone who wanders in for a friendly smile or an encouraging word.

According to Marsh, ministry to the racing community and ministry to the fans are significantly different worlds. But this doesn't mean that Raceway Ministries and MRO don't collaborate in their efforts from time to time. MRO often uses its influence with the drivers to coordinate appearances at Raceway Ministries community centers. Trevor Bayne, Blake Koch, and Michael McDowell are among those who have participated in autograph sessions and shared testimonies outside the garage. On the flip side, sometimes Raceway Ministries will use its vast connections in the various track locations to help MRO find musicians and worship leaders for its chapel services. Raceway Ministries and MRO also work together on chapel services for vendors.

"There's not a solid line of demarcation," Marsh says. "It's more of a dotted line. MRO typically serves the racing community. They do very well with it, and we respect them. Typically, we take care of the fans outside of the racing community itself. Speedways understand that. MRO understands that. We all just kind of respect each other's strengths, and then we borrow from each other when we need to mutually do an event that might require the strengths of each one of our groups."[15]

Ultimately, both Raceway Ministries and MRO share a common goal: to show God's love to others by serving others and meeting their physical, emotional, and spiritual needs. And just as MRO can share countless stories of what can happen as a result of that service, Raceway Ministries likewise can attest to the power of being present.

On Labor Day in 2011 Raceway Ministries volunteers were serving coffee and breakfast at Atlanta Motor Speedway in one of the ministry tents when a man walked in and sat down at one of the tables. He was dealing with some personal issues and just wanted someone with whom he could talk. For the next hour, the man shared his problems with one of Raceway Ministries volunteers. By the end of that conversation, the man had accepted Christ and then declared that he was leaving the track to go home and tell his family.[16]

A year earlier, at Texas Motor Speedway on a Saturday night, Marsh was involved in a similar encounter. He was setting up chairs for the next day's activities when, at about 10:30 p.m., three men walked into the tent. Marsh asked them if they needed help, but they said no. They then went to the literature table and asked if they could have some material.

Marsh proceeded to ask them if they were camping out or attending the race. They said no to both questions. They responded the same way when asked if they lived nearby. At that point, Marsh became understandably nervous and wary of their motives. But that all changed when they gathered around him and the youngest man spoke up.

"Three years ago I was here at one of your concerts," he said. "I was with my girlfriend. I was drunk. I was high. I was partying. I came over here and stood at the back and listened to what the singers had to say. I knew immediately I had to change. Something had to change. That prompted me to go back home and check into a drug rehab facility."

The young man identified one of the others with him as both the director of that facility and his pastor.

"I just wanted to bring my pastor here and show him where it all started," he added.[17]

Marsh says, "You never know what kind of impact you're having. This guy was on the periphery of a crowd watching a music concert, and yet it initiated something that changed his life. Much of what we do is like that. We do very little 'hard' evangelism. We mostly serve, and when we have an opportunity to share the gospel, we take that opportunity."[18]

Any Given Sunday

When most hardcore NASCAR fans start their Sunday, some might take time to visit church first, while others might be watching the early pre-race shows. But one thing is for sure: Most NASCAR fans probably are still in bed when ministry at the track gets underway.

For a typical Sunday afternoon race, Raceway Ministries hosts a chapel service for vendors as early as 6:30 a.m. The same is true for MRO, as Monty Self usually hosts a special gathering for members of the broadcast media.

By midmorning, it's time for the pre-race drivers' meeting, which is attended by all forty-three drivers and crew chiefs. At the end of the meeting the MRO chaplain on duty gives a closing prayer. As they dismiss, many of the drivers and crew chiefs head back to their garage areas, but several of them stay and are joined by crew members, family members, publicists, sponsors, NASCAR officials, and media members. Depending on the anticipated crowd, this might take place in a press conference room or somewhere larger, such as a vacated garage.

For the three hundred or so in attendance, the chapel service usually includes an opening and closing worship song with a devotional and offering squeezed in between. But most importantly, MRO provides NASCAR participants some semblance of church where otherwise there would be no such opportunity.

"It's tough to have any type of normal worship service or anywhere that you can go to and ask those tough questions because of our travel," driver David Ragan says. "I think it's great that Motor Racing Outreach and the people involved put out the effort to work with our busy schedules. A lot of drivers and their families count on them every weekend. It's been a blessing for us. It's a good thing to know that they're there for you throughout the weekend, whether you're in California, New Hampshire, or Daytona."[19]

As a Nationwide Series driver, Eric McClure usually attends the Saturday service, but he reaps the same benefits offered on Sunday.

"It's so important to me," he says. "I don't feel right racing if I haven't been in prayer. It's such an important part of my life. We have a good home church. But I love the MRO services. Those guys are encouragers for me. I can pick up the phone and call them if I have a problem. Other places may shove [spiritual things] out, but it's nice to be in a sport where there are a lot of people who believe the same way and [spiritual things] are embraced."[20]

As the service concludes, some drivers scamper away on golf carts to engagements required by their sponsors, while most crew members and crew chiefs in attendance meander back to their garage areas to prepare for the race. But it's common to see several people hanging around afterward. Michael McDowell, for instance, is a regular straggler who enjoys chatting with the chaplain or a fellow driver for as much time as he can spare. In many ways, it's no different than an average church service where people chat with friends before heading home to lunch.

But the mingling doesn't last for long. The main event is right around the corner, and the ramp-up can be just as entertaining. Pre-race concerts by national recording artists are the norm these days, and they precede the high-energy introductions of the drivers. The drivers are then driven around the track in the backseat of a convertible or in the bed of a pickup truck as they wave at fans and sometimes simultaneously conduct a live television interview for the national broadcast.

Once back at their race cars, drivers join their spouses and children or their significant others, along with sponsors and special guests. Then, the teams ceremoniously line up by their pit stalls and prepare for a rare moment of calm.

At every race a local minister or one of the ministry chaplains takes the microphone and offers a word of prayer. Sometimes a driver (such as Trevor Bayne) or an owner (such as Joe Gibbs) gives the invocation. Sometimes that prayer can even be controversial.

Former Cup chaplain Tim Griffin recalls such an instance in 2010 when he forgot to mention the troops in his prayer before a race in Phoenix. Griffin received several emails from fans that scolded him for the oversight.

And then there was the case of the infamous *Talladega Nights* prayer.

At the Nationwide Series race in Nashville on July 23, 2011, Pastor Joe Nelms, from Family Baptist Church in Lebanon, Tennessee, gave a rousing minute-long invocation that invoked Will Ferrell's "Ricky Bobby" character from the 2006 film comedy *Talladega Nights*. Nelms thanked a litany of sponsors (Sunoco fuel, Goodyear tires, and others) and manufacturers (Dodge, Toyota, Ford, General Motors) and made a chuckle-inducing reference to his "smokin' hot wife ... Lisa" and his two children, Eli and Emma, also known as "the Little E's."

Nelms then closed the prayer by paying tribute to both Darrell Waltrip and the Lord.

"In Jesus' name, boogity-boogity-boogity, amen!" he concluded.[21]

The prayer received mixed reactions, including a scathing review from ESPN writer David Newton, who called it "another black eye for a sport trying to distance itself from the hillbilly image that *Talladega Nights* played to the hilt."[22]

Dr. Jerry Punch, who was a pit road reporter at that race, would not go that far in his critique, but he did show concern for how Nelms's prayer might have negatively impacted public perception and the overall integrity of the pre-race tradition.

"It was funny," Punch admits. "But standing on pit road, I could hear drivers chuckling while the guy was doing it. In my opinion, prayer should be selfless. Prayer should be about someone else. In that situation, the individual made himself the star and not the one he was praying to. Prayer should be about being thankful for the blessings and what you've been given, and not being a stand-up comic. But, on the other hand, a lot of people turned to that website and went to his church the next Sunday. So maybe the ends did justify the means. I don't know."[23]

When questioned about the motivation behind his prayer, Nelms had this to say on Sirius Radio's *Tradin' Paint* program:

> I don't want to do the cookie-cutter prayer, not that we don't need to thank God for our military men and women. Absolutely, we wouldn't be here without them. Not that we don't desire safety for all of the officials, workers and drivers. We certainly don't want anything to happen to anybody out there. We need a safe race. But it's the same prayer week in and week out, and I'm not sure anybody is even listening to it anymore. So I said, "I want to get somebody's attention" … try to make an impact on the fans and give them something they'll remember and maybe they'll go home on a Friday night or a Saturday night and say, "Maybe I ought to get up and go to church in the morning."[24]

For the most part, however, the pre-race prayer goes off without a hitch and is always followed by the national anthem, usually sung by a national recording artist, although in recent years military veterans occasionally have performed the patriotic tune, while the MRO children's choir has become an annual tradition.

As the drivers say a few last words to their loved ones and friends, the chaplains scramble to finish a process that started during the introductions. Each driver is approached with an opportunity to receive a more personalized time of prayer. Sometimes it includes the driver's spouse. Other times, it includes the driver's crew chief. Sometimes, there's no prayer at all, but instead a simple "Good luck" for those who aren't exactly comfortable with the public expression of faith.

The chaplains try to catch the drivers before they get into their cars, but that doesn't always work out perfectly. This is especially the case with those who have qualified toward the front. Regardless of the situation, the prayer is something that most drivers embrace.

"Some of the guys want us to pray with them every week, and we know that ahead of time," Keller explains. "Some of them want prayer some weeks and don't want prayer other weeks. You just get a feel for it. Sometimes you can't get to everybody, but if you miss a driver for two weeks or more in a row, they let you know it. Some of the guys that want us to pray for them aren't church folks and maybe don't have a real fear of God in their life, but some of them have said to me more than once that it's a life-and-death sport, and they don't take it for granted. So there are a lot of guys that want the prayer just because of the nature of what they do."[25]

As pit road clears and the cars fire up their engines, the chaplains head back to the media room and watch the race as it unfolds on the television broadcast. They make sure to stay alert and be prepared for any incidents that might take place during the race. When the race is over, the MRO staff packs up the community center and heads back to the ministry headquarters in Charlotte. In just three days, the grinding process will start over again.

"There are days you walk around the garage, and you wonder if you're really making a difference," Billy Mauldin admits. "You start to question everything. But you can never do this more than a day at a time. You can't look back. You can't look forward.

You've got to take the day in front of you and do the best you can. In some cases, the fruit of our efforts may not be seen for another ten or twelve years. But as much as I want to see it happen today, the most important thing is that I just want to see them come to know the Lord before their earthly day is done."[26]

NOTES

1. Billy Mauldin, interview with the author, December 5, 2011.
2. Stephen Keller, interview with the author, October 9, 2011.
3. Ricky Stenhouse Jr., interview with the author, October 7, 2011.
4. Melanie Self, interview with the author, December 20, 2011.
5. Ibid.
6. Ibid.
7. Joe Nemechek, interview with the author, October 7, 2011.
8. Mark Martin, interview with the author, October 28, 2008.
9. Michael McDowell, interview with the author, October 1, 2010.
10. Ricky Stenhouse Jr., interview with the author, October 7, 2011.
11. Stephen Keller, interview with the author, October 9, 2011.
12. Ibid.
13. Ibid.
14. Dr. Roger Marsh, interview with the author, February 17, 2012.
15. Ibid.
16. Ibid.
17. Ibid.
18. Ibid.
19. David Ragan, interview with the author, October 31, 2008.
20. Eric McClure, interview with the author, November 6, 2009.
21. ESPN, *Federated Auto Parts 300*, July 23, 2011.
22. David Newton, "NASCAR Nationwide Series Prerace Prayer Another Black Eye for the Sport," ESPN Racing, July 26, 2011 (http://espn.go.com/racing/blog/_/name/newton_david/id/6804348/nascar-nationwide-series-prerace-prayer-another-black-eye-sport).
23. Dr. Jerry Punch, interview with the author, October 8, 2011.
24. Newton, "NASCAR Nationwide Series Prerace Prayer."
25. Stephen Keller, interview with the author, October 9, 2011.
26. Billy Mauldin, interview with the author, December 5, 2011.

CHAPTER 9

The Real Housewives of NASCAR

It wasn't quite midway through the 2003 season when Angie Skinner walked into the Motor Racing Outreach (MRO) community center at the end of a busy race weekend. Women's and children's director Melanie Self was going through her routine cleanup procedures. Skinner initially needed to talk to Self about one thing, but as soon as Skinner opened the door, Self could tell that something else was going on.

Self's assumption was correct. Skinner's husband, Mike, had just lost his ride in the Cup Series. Morgan-McClure Motorsports had released him after the sixteenth race of the 2003 season, where he failed to qualify for the Sirius 400 at Michigan International Speedway.

"I told her to come sit by me," Self recalls. "[Angie] began to share her struggles. My heart broke for her, and we prayed together."[1]

Mike Skinner was trying to decide whether or not to go back to the Truck Series, where his NASCAR career was launched. Not long after that impromptu prayer meeting he was given the chance to drive for Billy Ballew Motorsports. Later in the season he got behind the wheel for MBV Motorsports and then Michael Waltrip

Racing. Skinner then spent the next eight years flourishing with Toyota Racing.

So impacted by her time with Self, Angie Skinner returned later that same year with another driver's wife to have the exact same conversation.

"Tell her what you told me," Skinner prompted Self.

"You need to listen to what Miss Melanie has to say," Skinner then said to her companion. "Because this is important!"[2]

Motorsports Matriarchs

Conversations such as the one between Melanie Self and Angie Skinner have been taking place in the infield well before the actual existence of track ministry. Stock car racing has always been a tough sport, and the men behind it have always relied heavily on their spouses for emotional and spiritual support. In turn, the wives have traditionally turned to one another and to organizations such MRO for their own emotional and spiritual needs.

Amy Gordon is married to Penske Racing crew chief Todd Gordon, who during the 2013 season worked for Joey Logano's #22 team. Also the mother of two young daughters, she fully understands the difficulties that her husband faces every day.

"This is a very precarious business," Gordon says. "You never really know if your husband is going to have a job the following year. Usually you find out around December. That is a challenge. There's a lot of pressure on Todd all the time. He just works. He'll come home really late at night, and he leaves early in the morning. We've known this kind of world for so long that it seems normal to us."[3]

The sport's familial nature started to develop in the 1960s and continued to evolve during the 1970s, thanks to drivers such as Richard Petty, Bobby Allison, and Darrell Waltrip. It was normal during those eras for men to travel alone. In fact, women and anyone under the age of twenty-one were not allowed in the pits. But eventually, thanks to drivers who yearned for a more normal existence, the culture slowly began to change into more of a family-friendly environment.

Lynda Petty, Judy Allison, and Stevie Waltrip are considered notable matriarchs of motorsports ministry. They supported the presence of Bill Frazier and Bill Baird and encouraged their husbands to remain active in chapel at the track and in church back home. They were also working behind the scenes to create a sense of community among the wives.

"When [Stevie] was at the racetrack, she was homeschooling the girls," former Cup chaplain Dale Beaver says. "She was just always very approachable and had a real pastor's heart, a shepherd's heart for these women. As a result of that, she had a lot of influence on a lot of girls."[4]

Shortly after MRO was launched in 1988, it became clear that there was a need for targeted ministry for women and children. Those two areas were combined and put under the care of Jackie Pegram, or Miss Jackie, as she would quickly become known. In 1998 Melanie Self began working with MRO and joined the staff fulltime in 2001. Her husband, Monty, was a career military man, and once he retired, he too decided that the NASCAR-affiliated ministry was the next logical step. By 2006, Pegram had retired and turned over the reigns to Self, who remains in that capacity today.

"Every part of our military lifestyle became clearly evident within the motorsports community," Self says. "Early on in the ministry, we worked on building relationships. Our scope has changed through the years. There is a third generation of children coming through MRO programming. As that's changed, we've had to shape and mold ourselves to fit the needs of the women and children."[5]

Those changes have translated into increased support for wives and girlfriends via free childcare during the races, Bible studies, reading clubs, and opportunities for ministry and community at home away from the track. MRO hosts two annual events for women, including the preseason January Caution, a gathering that allows wives to reflect on the past season and prepare emotionally and spiritually for the upcoming season, and the Summer Caution, an outreach that gives wives the opportunity to partner with various humanitarian programs.

"Working with the NASCAR community is like being (a missionary) in Africa," Self says. "We've been grafted in. They allow us the privilege to be here. The favor of God has allowed us to have a footprint in the neighborhood. We don't take that for granted. So they're not going to understand the words I use and the terminology. We don't talk church-like. We are an outreach. I'm after these women's hearts. I want to make sure they know Christ."[6]

Taking the Lead

Although men have historically filled the pastoral role at a majority of churches, it often is the women who drive much of the evangelism and community outreach, and, in general, tend to show more interest in church activities. Studies show that church attendance has steadily declined over the past forty to fifty years, but still, women in the United States are 8 to 10 percent more likely to consistently attend a weekly church service than are men.[7]

So it shouldn't be a surprise that women are typically the driving force behind the faith of NASCAR's leading men. As this reality became clear to MRO's leadership during the 1990s and early 2000s, chaplains such as Dale Beaver became more intentional about equipping the wives to plant the seeds of spiritual growth within their marriages.

"The women tend to be the steady companion," concurs MRO president Billy Mauldin. "These guys go through so many ups and downs and adrenaline rushes and pressures of competition and career fluctuations. A lot of these ladies are behind the scenes. They have to be there for them and absorb a lot of that stuff. The women help these men manage the ups and downs and help them deal with it. So they need a constant in their life, and the ones that are most successful at it tend to have a level of faith and a relationship with Christ. As they walk through these seasons of life with these men, the women remain steady, and the men see that. That causes the men to make changes in their lives, particularly when they get older."[8]

In some cases, it's the wife who directly impacts the husband's initial experience with God. Nationwide Series driver Eric McClure can attest to this reality. As someone who had resisted exposing himself to the Christian lifestyle, it took a strong interest in a young woman to open his heart to spiritual matters.

"I wanted to date my wife, Miranda, for a long time," McClure says. "She was the beauty queen. She was the head cheerleader. I had this huge desire to date her. I finally got a huge wave of confidence, and I asked her out. So we went out, and sure enough, the day after we went out, she invited me to church. And it was awful."[9]

McClure endured three years of attending church and not wanting to fully embrace the gospel message. But not long after his wedding, McClure accepted Christ following a church service where some teenage baseball players had shared about their experiences at camp. His wife's patience and prayer made all the difference.

In other cases, the spiritual growth within a couple's life might take place simultaneously, but with Nationwide Series driver Justin Allgaier, it's what happens when success comes where the spouse's role becomes that much more important. Allgaier and his wife, Ashley, met when they were fifteen years old. They got married when they were just nineteen. Justin had already been racing ten years by the time they met, but he's thankful that she's been by his side throughout his entire NASCAR career.

"I probably wouldn't be in the situation I'm in if it wasn't for Ashley," Allgaier says. "It helps me a lot [to be married]. I can't imagine being in this sport being single. It's been good for me to have someone there. My wife's not my biggest cheerleader. She's probably my biggest critic most of the time. She helps balance out who I am, what I do, and how I need to get it done. That's huge."[10]

The same holds true for Sprint Cup driver Michael McDowell. He and his wife, Jami, married in 2001, but they didn't become Christians until 2005. McDowell feels blessed to have someone in his life who understands every aspect of his life.

"We've gone through this whole process together—the struggles, the high points, the low points," he says. "Trying to break into this sport is extremely difficult. There are a lot of tough times through that process. She really gets it. She knows as much about the sport as I do. She understands how hard it is. It's been an amazing journey to have that support and have somebody that not only believes in your ability, but also shares the same faith and passion and pursuit. Jami is that constant, just like how God is there. He's always the same loving God. So having a spouse that's in it with you is awesome."[11]

Girlfriend Power

Sometimes NASCAR wives first show up on the scene as just that, wives. But with so many young drivers getting into the sport as teenagers and young adults, a good portion of these significant others are first introduced as girlfriends or fiancées. Katie Kenseth, Chandra Johnson, and Nicole Biffle are three prominent examples of women who married their husbands well into their NASCAR careers. In all circumstances, Self says that MRO has always provided them a safe place of acceptance and acclimation.

"Being a girlfriend out there is a little different," she says. "You're not in, but you're not out. What do you call that? It's just an odd place."[12]

Self met Nicole Biffle early in Nicole's relationship with Greg. After the couple's long courtship and engagement, Self says that it was "wonderful" to be able to attend their wedding as "a completion of the investment" she had made into Nicole's life.[13]

While most of those situations tend to play out in the background and away from the public eye, that certainly wasn't the case with Patricia Driscoll. On June 24, 2011, the Sprint Cup series was at Infineon Raceway in Sonoma, California. During TNT's pre-race coverage of the national anthem, cameras cut to a shot of Kurt Busch, who was standing by Driscoll. This created somewhat of a stir because most race fans were unaware that Kurt's marriage to Eva Busch had effectively ended months earlier.

It was an awkward entry into the NASCAR spotlight, one that Driscoll would not have imagined the first time she met Busch a few years earlier. As the CEO of the Armed Forces Foundation, Driscoll was present when Busch visited Walter Reed Army Medical Center. She was surprised to find that Kurt was much different from how he had been portrayed in the media.

"What's written about Kurt is not at all the person that he is," Driscoll says. "They love to focus on the negative side. They love to take his statements out of context. He's actually really pretty funny. Sometimes his jokes don't come across very well, but he's a competitor at heart."[14]

Although Driscoll and Busch had kept their relationship private until that moment at Sonoma, they had already been taking advantage of MRO's presence at the track, including chapel services and children's ministry for Driscoll's son, Houston. But more importantly, MRO provided safe haven during a time when Driscoll was going through a nasty divorce and custody battle of her own.

"MRO has always been very loving and supportive," she says. "This was before I even knew Kurt. I spent a lot of time at the track because of our relationship with NASCAR. The Armed Forces Foundation is NASCAR's official military charity. We bring troops to the track, and Houston would come with me a lot. Both Houston and I had difficulties going through the divorce. They were there to see us through that."[15]

In fact, MRO helped Driscoll deal with the aftermath of her personal struggles. When her ex-husband was attempting to gain full custody of Houston, her friends within the ministry organization reminded her to look past the hurt and think about what was best for her son.

"They were there for me when I was angry and weak and just ready to play all my cards and take [my ex-husband] out," Driscoll says. "I could have done that, but I chose not to because of MRO's advice. They were right. They've given me a lot of guidance."[16]

Ultimately, her ex-husband backed away from his demands, and joint custody was granted. And although that firestorm was over, Driscoll faced a different kind of heat when her and Busch's relationship became public. At that point, trust and confidentiality became the most important thing that MRO could offer.

"MRO has always given us that safe place to be," Driscoll says. "We can be ourselves. We can talk about our real, everyday problems. They don't treat us any different."[17]

The Good Ol' Girls Club

Once relegated to the background, the wives and girlfriends have now become a visible part of the NASCAR community. This fact was especially obvious when MRO organized a new event in 2011 called "The Better Half Dash."

The event was held at Charlotte Motor Speedway in October of that year. Fourteen women took to the front stretch quarter-mile in Bandolero cars[18] as a fundraiser for MRO and Speedway Children's Charities. The inaugural race included Ashley Allgaier, Patricia Driscoll, Michelle Gilliland (wife of David Gilliland), Shannon Koch (wife of Blake Koch), Jami McDowell, Tricia

Mears (wife of Casey Mears), Melanie Self, Angie Skinner, Kristen Yeley (wife of J. J. Yeley), and Nan Zipadelli (wife of Greg Zipadelli). The event returned in 2012 and featured several of the original competitors as well as newcomers such as Kris Buescher (wife of James Buescher), Amy Gordon, and Lyn-Z Pastrana (wife of Travis Pastrana).

For McDowell, her participation in the 2011 race was another opportunity to bond with some other wives who hold the same values and beliefs.

"There are a lot of women in the sport that are living real life," she says. "They're there to support their husbands and keep their family together, and they're living a real Christian walk. Those are the women that I definitely cling to and choose to associate with."[19]

When McDowell's husband, Michael, and some other young drivers, including Trevor Bayne, Justin Allgaier, Blake Koch, and Ricky Stenhouse Jr., started meeting together on Saturday mornings for Bible studies at the track, she and the other wives took note.

"We were seeing such growth in our husbands, and we were a little jealous of that and wanted some of that for ourselves," McDowell says. "But we don't all travel to the same races. Some of us are on the Cup circuit and others are on the Nationwide circuit. A lot of it also came from me wanting to have a connection with the other women. So we decided to take what [the men] had and add the wives and whoever else was interested and get together as a group during the week. It's created a real sense of community. Now when we're at the track, it's easier for [the women] to get together because we already have that at home, and we can trust each other. We know each other better now. It's easier for us to reach out and say 'Let's get together' than it was before."[20]

Driscoll can relate to the importance of connecting with other women at the tracks. This is especially true when it comes to her desire to grow in her faith. That's why the activities and community outreach events have been so invaluable.

"Life is like an ongoing high school," Driscoll says. "The drivers' lot is no different. I just feel like a lot of that stuff goes away with MRO. We're all on the same page. [MRO has] been that equalizer for all of us. That brings more friendships, and it means that people are letting go of some of those old rules."21

Godly Muscle

While the drivers' wives have long been a staple within the NASCAR garage, another group of women has increasingly made its presence felt, albeit at a pace that often seems painstakingly slow. Teri MacDonald-Cadieux is one of those women who found their way onto the track and behind the wheel of a high-powered stock car. She experienced the struggle to fit in from a completely different perspective.

"When I went into NASCAR, I was underfunded, I came from a road racing background, and I was a woman," she says. "So those were three marks against me. That was hard to deal with. You walk into a room with a bunch of guys, and you either stand by yourself or you go to a circle and hope you're accepted in that circle."22

MacDonald-Cadieux first hit the scene as a road racer with International Motor Sports Association and as an Indy Car pace car driver with the PPG Pace Car Team. While racing at the 1997 Road Atlanta event, she hit the wall at 160-miles per hour and rolled her car multiple times. As a result, MacDonald-Cadieux broke her C2 vertebrae in three places. She was put into a halo device and required to wear a body cast for 13 weeks. Incredibly, she now sees that tragic event as one of the best things that ever happened to her.

"It got the focus off myself and back on to God," MacDonald-Cadieux says. "Racing had become my god. I still loved Jesus, but he had gone into my back pocket. He was there, but only when I really needed him. So that accident was really a wakeup call. It helped me realize that I wasn't here to glorify myself but to glorify God. That's when I started to make a daily, focused commitment to keep [Jesus] on the throne and put him first in my life."[23]

That renewed relationship with Christ helped her prepare for the challenges that accompanied her attempt to break into the NASCAR ranks. After competing in 13 NASCAR Canadian Tire Series races during 2001 and 2002, MacDonald-Cadieux made the jump to the NASCAR Truck Series where she qualified for seven races over three years.

During that time, she twice made history. In 2002 at Memphis Motorsports Park, she and brother Randy MacDonald become just the second brother-sister combination to qualify for a top-level NASCAR race. The previous happening was in 1949 when Tim Flock and his sister Ethyl Flock Mobley both made a Grand National Series start.

In 2004, she qualified in the Truck Series along with Tina Gordon and Kelly Sutton at the UAW/GM Ohio 250 in Mansfield, Ohio. That marked the first time that three female drivers had started the same race in one of NASCAR's main three series. It was also at that race where MacDonald-Cadieux learned a hard lesson about gender equity in the sport.

"Jack Sprague knocked all three of us out of the race individually," she explains. "First he hit Tina and took her out. Then he hit me. Then he hit Kelly. All of us had crash marks from the same guy. Afterward, we just had to laugh about it. There are some drivers that accept you and totally include you and treat you like an equal, and then there are the other ones that spin you out when they need to get a caution flag. Those guys look at you as dispensable. You're just a pylon on the race track to them."[24]

Discouraged but undaunted, MacDonald-Cadieux made a commitment to use the platform for as long as it was available. Under the guidance of Dr. Roger Marsh (Raceway Ministries) and Bill Carpenter (MRO), she and brother Randy spoke frequently during NASCAR weekend at churches, schools, conferences, and events at the track.

"We were kind of the pioneers of that kind of ministry because we were so willing to go wherever we were asked to go," she says. "We were speaking sometimes two or three times a weekend. From there, we were able to mentor Michael McDowell, who has gone on to do a lot of speaking of his own. And since then, Michael has become a mentor to Trevor Bayne. It's been an awesome ripple effect."[25]

But when it comes to her racing career, MacDonald-Cadieux looks back and can't help but have the occasional bitter taste in her mouth. Female drivers have been trying to break into the sport since 1949, yet only a handful lasted longer than a season or two. Janet Guthrie was one of the most notable exceptions. By the time she retired in 1976, she had started 33 races at the Cup level. Patty Moise provided another bright spot in the late 1980s when she made 133 races in the Nationwide (then Busch) Series. And, of course, Danica Patrick has set a new standard and hope for a more diverse future.

Still, MacDonald-Cadieux remains skeptical and often wonders if the glass ceiling will ever truly break.

"I don't know if it's possible," she says. "To be honest, I can't see it happening. I don't think there's enough money, enough talent, or enough open doors right now. Danica is doing a fantastic job breaking a lot of barriers. She's got the media on her side. She's got NASCAR on her side. She's doing everything she can do to raise the awareness. But it's still not enough."[26]

And for those female drivers who keep fighting for relevancy and equal opportunity within NASCAR, MacDonald-Cadieux has a piece of spiritual advice that comes from her years of experiencing the same set of challenges.

"Any time you are a female in a man's sport, it's a struggle," she says. "You're going against the current. It's going to be an uphill battle. You're going to need a lot of godly muscle to get through that."[27]

NOTES

1. Melanie Self, interview with the author, December 20, 2011.
2. Ibid.
3. Amy Gordon, interview with the author, October 5, 2012.
4. Dale Beaver, interview with the author, August 21, 2012.
5. Melanie Self, interview with the author, December 20, 2011.
6. Ibid.
7. "20 Years of Surveys Show Key Differences in the Faith of America's Men and Women," Barna Group, August 1, 2011 (https://www.barna.org/barna-update/faith-spirituality/508-20-years-of-surveys-show-key-differences-in-the-faith-of-americas-men-and-women).
8. Billy Mauldin, interview with the author, December 5, 2011.
9. Eric McClure, interview with the author, November 6, 2009.
10. Justin Allgaier, interview with the author, January 17, 2012.
11. Michael McDowell, interview with the author, October 1, 2010.
12. Melanie Self, interview with the author, December 20, 2011.
13. Ibid.
14. Patricia Driscoll, interview with the author, September 29, 2012.
15. Ibid.
16. Ibid.
17. Ibid.
18. Bandolero cars are built like miniature stock cars. They reach up to seventy miles per hour and are used primarily as entry-level vehicles for drivers between the ages of eight and sixteen.
19. Jami McDowell, interview with the author, February 15, 2012.
20. Ibid.
21. Patricia Driscoll, interview with the author, September 29, 2012.
22. Teri MacDonald-Cadieux, interview with the author, July 1, 2013.
23. Ibid.
24. Ibid.
25. Ibid.
26. Ibid.
27. Ibid.

CHAPTER 10

Kids' Play

In a lot of ways, NASCAR is really just a bunch of grown-up kids playing with their toys. Of course, real kids don't have 3,400-pound life-size cars that cost upwards of $200,000 and go two hundred miles per hour, and they don't play with forty-two other kids and their life-size cars. But in essence, NASCAR is a grownup sport with a childlike mentality—go fast, go hard, go in circles.

It so happens that many of the drivers have young children, or have children who are now young adults, or will likely have kids in the near future. Because of that cyclical fact of life, MRO has maintained some level of children's ministry since its inception. Therefore, kids' ministry at the track has impacted most everyone inside the motor coach lot at some point in time. Phil Parsons's oldest daughter, Kensley, was one of the first kids to attend what became known as the Bible Club. The boom continued throughout the 1990s and early 2000s, with beneficiaries that included Mark Martin's son Matt, Larry McReynolds's son Brandon, Terry Labonte's son Justin, Robert Pressley's son Coleman, and Joe Nemechek's son John Hunter and daughter Blair.

But when drivers with children such as Jimmy Spencer and Ward Burton retired, and the previously mentioned offspring (Parsons, Martin, McReynolds, Labonte, Pressley, and Nemecheck) became teenagers and young adults, there was a lessened need for children's ministry, and the Bible Club was scaled back for a few years. That all changed when many of the young single drivers, including Matt Kenseth and Jimmie Johnson, got married and starting having children. This trend has continued with Jeff Gordon, Carl Edwards, Sam Hornish Jr., Casey Mears, Greg Biffle, and several others.

As drivers experience a new reality, there are unique opportunities created for Motor Racing Outreach (MRO) in which the organization is able to serve not only the children, but their parents as well.

"When you're single, you don't mix and mingle as much," MRO president Billy Mauldin says. "But when you start having kids, that really enables us to bring those people out to our family events. When you have community, that's really the setting that helps with spiritual growth. You add to that the kids that bring in their stories of what they're learning, and God takes all of this stuff and weaves it together like a patchwork quilt to create a finished product. It takes all of us. As a ministry, you could just send a chaplain, but a chaplain can only do so much. That's why we add other elements, like family ministry. We have all of these pieces, and it takes a lot of people working together both directly and indirectly to see the things happen in these people's lives that are genuine transformations."[1]

Divine Daycare

Once NASCAR participants buy into MRO's relevance to their family's life, the door is open for them to reap the benefits of what essentially starts out as daycare and then grows into something much more significant. Mostly utilized by drivers and crew chiefs, MRO's community center opens the door to life's big picture.

"When these guys start to have kids, their perspectives start to change to some degree," Mauldin says. "They begin to look at life with that added responsibility as well as the joy that comes with it. These drivers are constantly on the go and constantly on the road. So there's a real level of concern about what's happening with their kids. Are they growing up right? Historically, a lot of them have seen MRO as a resource to help them make sure that their kids are getting the things they think they need to get."[2]

MRO knows that it has competition. Most of the drivers and many of the crew chiefs have pricey motor homes that feature all the electronic gadgets a kid would ever want. So while the ministry makes sure to stock the community center with video games and toys, the most important elements remain intangible by nature.

"Our heart is to make sure we give them attention and invest in them so they'll want to be around us," MRO women's and children's ministry coordinator Melanie Self says. "That was the heritage that started years ago. The paradigm has changed somewhat from that, but the same principle applies. 'Hey, if you love my kid, I'm gonna love you.' We truly look at these kids as our neighbors and our friends."[3]

On a typical race weekend, Self and other staff members schedule Friday, Saturday, and Sunday with fun things for the children. They have plenty of snacks on hand and wall-to-wall activities. Sometimes that even includes interaction with the parents after the practice laps and qualifying runs have been completed. Watermelon-eating contests, relay races, access to kiddie pools, and special events such as the Father's Day Olympics are just a few things that take place within the community center's confines and its surrounding area.

"We're very conscious of the protection and care of the community," Self says. "Our number one buzzword is 'safe haven.' I will put my body between a child and anything that might harm them, whether that's a vehicle or a golf cart or a [suspicious] person trying to pick them up. It's the same thing you'd expect in a neighborhood or a daycare. The difference is that you know we'll provide Bible programming."[4]

Patricia Driscoll has long appreciated MRO's services for her son, Houston. In the past, she brought him to the track when accompanying military veterans to races on behalf of the Armed Forces Foundation. More recently, the two have begun attending events in support of Driscoll's boyfriend, Kurt Busch.

"MRO is an extended family for Houston," Driscoll says. "He really looks forward to coming to the track every weekend, not just because he loves cars and racing, but because he loves his friends. MRO gives him a place to play. That's very important for a little boy. He has that love and support every time he comes to the track. He's never bored. And [during the 2012 season], he got to race toy cars with Carl Edwards. What kid gets that opportunity? But if it weren't for MRO having their motor home in the lot and being there every weekend, a lot of us probably wouldn't be out traveling as much with our kids. That's really something special."[5]

On race day, many of the children go to pit road to be with their parents during the pre-race ceremonies. But by the time the green flag drops, they are already inside the community center again, getting ready to start Bible Club activities. At the Homestead race during the 2011 season, Self recalls keeping the kids for six hours due to multiple wrecks.

"What do you do for six hours?" Self rhetorically asks. "You've got to be ready if you're going to have them for an hour and a half or six hours. You keep pulling rabbits out of your hat. But the reality is, if they're with you for the weekend, the lull created from the hum of the engines provides an environment for us to worship and sing. They'll sit there for two hours listening to stories. I'll teach them as long as they will listen—truths about life based on biblical principles."[6]

Self always opens with prayer. She and her assistant first ask for special requests and then take time to pray with each child.

Sometimes those prayers address difficult things that their family is facing. Other times, they are celebrating good things that have happened during the week.

"This becomes a time when they open up their hearts," Self adds. "Most of the time we're praying for safety. They're very aware that [racing is] dangerous."[7]

Self became acutely aware of that fact after Dale Earnhardt Sr. died in 2001. That same season, one child came to her and explained, "If Earnhardt can die, anyone can die."[8]

Self does her best to shield the children from what's going on with the race. But when the cars stop on the track, even the youngest in the room are savvy enough to know that something isn't quite right. When an accident takes place, Self stops what she's doing and waits for her husband, Monty, to stop by and let her know what's going on.

She remembers one incident in particular where it was obvious to her that everything was fine, but the driver's son had been watching the coverage and was very upset.

"Is the window net down?" the little boy astutely asked.

"See, the window net *is* down," Self replied.

"That's good, right?" he asked.

"Yes, your daddy did that," she calmly reassured.

Self and the child continued to watch the coverage as the driver waved at the crowd and climbed into the ambulance. The boy was then escorted to see his dad. When he came back a few minutes later, he walked in the room and gave everyone the thumbs-up sign. His dad was just fine.

"We make sure to remind them that these cars are safer than any cars anywhere," Self says. "They don't have to worry about what happened to Dale Earnhardt. We remind them about the HANS device[9] and how it connects to their dads' neck's and holds them real stiff. We try to create calm for them."[10]

Elementary Evangelism

On the morning of the 2001 Daytona 500, then Cup chaplain Dale Beaver and Cup driver Michael Waltrip were engaged in a casual conversation when Waltrip made an unusual promise. If he won the race, he would sing the popular children's song "This Is the Day" in Victory Lane during his national media interview.

Beaver was taken aback by Waltrip's declaration, but he quickly understood the nature of its origin.

"If your kid was at the track at the children's program, these kids either reached their parents for Christ or they added to the discipleship these folks were taking part in," Beaver explains. "The kids learned songs, and then they'd be singing these songs on trips and to the store. Those songs get in the back of your head."[11]

The events that took place later that afternoon would be forever etched in NASCAR history. Dale Earnhardt Sr. pushed his teammates, Waltrip and Dale Earnhardt Jr., to a one-two finish, but tragically he was killed in an accident that ensued on the final lap. Waltrip, still unaware of what had happened to his team owner, got out of his car and conducted a post-race interview with Fox Sports reporter Dick Berggren. After a few minutes of excitement, he finally let out the first line of that song he had learned from his three-year old daughter, Macy.

"This is the day that the Lord has made!" he proclaimed.

"I never will forget that," Beaver says. "He got to Victory Lane and forgot the words. But he ended up quoting it. I find it interesting that the day Dale was killed, Michael was thinking about that kids' song. It just seemed to be a providential thing."[12]

When Waltrip brought a piece of Macy's MRO experience into the public square, it was proof that the Bible Club and other activities from the community center were more than just kids' play. The NASCAR children clearly were having an impact on their parents' spiritual journeys. Michael Waltrip's older brother, Darrell, can certainly attest to that fact. He was greatly challenged by his daughters, Jessica and Sarah, who were homeschooled by his wife, Stevie, and influenced by MRO's presence at the track.

"Over the years, there have been kids who have gone back to their motor coaches after the race or on their way home and led their moms and dads to Christ because of what they learned in the Bible Club," Darrell Waltrip says. "Kids would really put their moms and dads on the spot."[13]

One of the more recent examples took place with Hendrick Motor Sports crew chief Steve Letarte. As regular attendees of the Bible Club, his children, Tyler and Ashlyn, began going home after the race weekends and telling him and his wife, Tricia, what they had learned.

"Steve began to become very convicted that he didn't know the answers that his children knew," Self says.[14]

Letarte decided that something needed to change, so he enrolled in a religion class at his church in Huntersville, North Carolina. As Letarte began to grow in his Bible knowledge, he realized that he did not have the same relationship with God that his kids had been talking about. Within a year, Letarte had allowed the process to completely transform his life. At the second Bristol race of the 2011 season, Tricia Letarte informed Self that her husband was going to be baptized soon. The couple wanted her to be there to witness the occasion.

"Wives can say a lot of things, but the kids will get to you," Self says. "They're not trying to force anything on you. They're just talking about how cool these stories are. It's been very wonderful to watch this family grow before our very eyes."[15]

According to Mauldin, the key is when parents see "something different in their kids." As they begin to pinpoint the Bible Club as the source of that positive change, it helps open their hearts to the gospel.[16]

"A lot of the guys who have sworn off anything God-related, their kids will end up coming to the MRO children's area," Cup chaplain Stephen Keller explains. "Suddenly conversations begin. Or their wives will get involved with some of the other wives, and then *the men* will want to go to chapel. A lot of times, it's either the kids or the wives that end up bringing the whole family together. The next thing you know, there are guys that seemed like a lost cause that are walking with the Lord with their whole family."[17]

At times, the child's impact goes outside the walls of the home and reaches into some unlikely places. In 2005, for instance, Self was teaching the Bible Club about what it means to be in the Lord's army. The lesson focused on Joshua, the man who took charge of the Israelites after Moses had died. On one particular race weekend, Joshua 3:5 was the verse for the day: "Consecrate yourself to the LORD, for tomorrow the LORD will do wonders among you."

"I told the children that the message was theirs. It wasn't just mine," Self says. "I told them that as we grow and as we learn, we are responsible to share that with other people."[18]

Self could see right away that Greg Zipadelli's oldest son, Zach, was especially gripped by the story. As she explained the meaning of the word *consecrate* and the importance of carefully following God's instructions, the six-year-old took to heart Self's prayer that encouraged the kids to tell someone what they had learned that afternoon.

"Unbeknownst to me, his family would be flying with the driver that his dad worked for at this time," she says. "They spent a few hours on the plane, and the entire time [Zach] sat with this driver and told him every part of Joshua's life."[19]

"Do you believe it?" the young Zipadelli asked the man.

At the next race, Self ran into the driver and the two had a humorous, if not revealing, exchange.

"[*Expletive!*] What do you teach those kids?" he said.

"I teach them what I believe and what I know is truth for their lives," she replied.

The driver let out another profane expression as he smiled and shook his head.

"[The driver and I] now have a forever-forged friendship because we believe in what we do enough to come and do what we do," Self says.[20]

Beyond the child-directed evangelism that emerges from MRO's community center, Self also points to the individual spiritual growth that takes place in so many of her students' hearts. During the 2005 season at a race weekend in Richmond, Virginia, she shared with the kids that her eighty-six-year-old grandmother was going to die soon. Self asked the class to pray that she would be at peace and pain-free before going to heaven. That's when Jeff Burton's daughter, Paige, spoke up.

"No," Paige said as she took Self's hand. "I'm going to pray for *you*!"[21]

It was a touching moment as the ten-year-old girl proceeded to pray for her teacher.

"Eternal things go on in those quiet moments when forty-three cars zoom around our heads," Self says. "It makes no sense that those kids would sit there and listen. Yet we meet God in that place, and it gets to a point where you don't hear the race cars anymore. I don't even understand it. Well, it must be the Holy Spirit."[22]

NOTES
1. Billy Mauldin, interview with the author, December 5, 2011.
2. Ibid.
3. Melanie Self, interview with the author, December 20, 2011.
4. Ibid.
5. Patricia Driscoll, interview with the author, September 29, 2012.
6. Melanie Self, interview with the author, December 20, 2011.
7. Ibid.
8. Ibid.
9. The (HANS) device, or "head and neck support," is an apparatus that is attached to the driver's helmet and stops the head from whipping forward during a crash.
10. Melanie Self, interview with the author, December 20, 2011.
11. Dale Beaver, interview with the author, August 21, 2012.
12. Ibid.

13. Darrell Waltrip, interview with the author, October 2, 2010.
14. Melanie Self, interview with the author, December 20, 2011.
15. Ibid.
16. Billy Mauldin, interview with the author, December 5, 2011.
17. Stephen Keller, interview with the author, October 9, 2011.
18. Melanie Self, interview with the author, December 20, 2011.
19. Ibid.
20. Ibid.
21. Ibid.
22. Ibid.

CHAPTER 11

Back at the Shop

For the three thousand or so individuals who travel the NASCAR circuit each week, there are thousands more who never go to the track. In reality, the vast majority of those employed by NASCAR and its various race teams stay home for the weekend after working long hours back at the shop.

Nick Terry knows a little something about that lifestyle. He spent ten years as a crew member for Richard Childress Racing (RCR) and saw firsthand the laborious effort that goes into making it possible for drivers to be successful.

"There's a lot that goes into getting these cars to the racetrack," Terry says. "Some of the stuff that shop guys live through is really stressful. It's a high-pressure environment. You've always got to do better. You've always got to be looking forward. You never have the opportunity in the sport to look back and go, 'Ah, man, we did good last week!' because last week really doesn't count anymore."[1]

In 2012 Terry took his experience as a jack man for drivers such as Kevin Harvick and Clint Bowyer into a new role as Nationwide series chaplain. He brought with him the understanding that those who travel to the races and those who don't have the exact same spiritual needs.

"There's a definite need for ministry for the people that are in the sport," Terry explains. "It's just about teaching guys or just reassuring them that you can love God in this environment. It's very competitive, and it's hard to break down walls sometimes. It's hard for them to say, 'I'm going to humble myself and take a stand for Christ.' But it can be done."2

The Trickle-Down Effect

Even though most race team employees are available to attend church services on Sunday and other ministry activities during the week, outreach efforts back at the shops are still vitally important. Some of the larger teams, like Joe Gibbs Racing (JGR), have full-time chaplains who tend to their employees' spiritual and emotional needs. Several others allow for pastors, ministers, or even staff volunteers to hold weekly Bible studies on their campus.

RCR, for example, brought in Richard Payne to be the shop chaplain. He trained some of the team members, including Terry and more recently pit crew member Ray Wright, to take the reins. Hendrick Motor Sports (HMS) has also been known for its support of home base ministry. Rick Hendrick's younger brother John held a Bible study for HMS employees up until he was tragically killed in a 2004 plane crash along with his twin daughters and eight others, including Rick's only son, Ricky.

Just as NASCAR's support of track site ministry validates the presence of Motor Racing Outreach (MRO) and Raceway Ministries, so too does the support of Christian team owners when it comes to efforts back at the shop. But their value and influence extends well beyond those confines in what could be described as a trickle-down effect.

Randy MacDonald isn't a high-profile owner like Rick Hendrick or Richard Petty. He's just a former driver trying to fulfill a lifelong dream within the world of stock car racing. After making 131 NASCAR starts over twelve years, MacDonald took on the role of owner in 2008. His quiet influence made a difference in the lives of drivers such as Michael McDowell and Blake Koch.

"Randy has so much faith," Koch says. "He doesn't get upset. He keeps his cool. He also shows love and compassion. He's really such a sensitive guy and a loving person. If I needed anything from Randy, he'd be there. I could come in and be so upset because the car's not good, and on top of that I could've just wrecked the car, and Randy still shows love and humility. It's not all about racing for Randy. He wants to have an effective outreach off the racetrack."[3]

On the other hand, there is the highly recognizable Joe Gibbs, a championship-winning owner with an impeccable record of integrity and success across two major professional sports, football and auto racing. Not long after starting JGR in 1991, he invited chaplain Bob Dyar to spend one day a week at the race shop and begin mentoring anyone on his staff who was interested in learning more about the Bible or growing in faith. Eventually, Dyar became the full-time staff chaplain and developed a program that includes a Wednesday Bible study and intensive discipleship efforts.

Former MRO chaplain Lonnie Clouse has seen Gibbs's commitment to workplace evangelism up close and personal. Before joining MRO, Clouse was a residential counselor at Gibbs's Youth For Tomorrow home in Washington, DC. It was Gibbs, in fact, who wrote the letter of recommendation for Clouse when he took a position with MRO in 1999.

"He's definitely one of those guys who doesn't just say it; he lives it and believes it," Clouse says. "For Joe, it's not about winning championships. It's about bringing honor and glory to the Lord. You can see it in the people that he's surrounded himself with and the leadership at Joe Gibbs Racing. Those guys are sold out and passionate about their relationship with Jesus Christ. It's a great working environment that lets the light of Christ shine."[4]

Not shy about sharing his faith in the public square, Gibbs has occasionally led the pre-race prayer for Cup events, and he always makes sure to leave an impression on anyone he meets.

"It doesn't take long to figure out that Joe is the real deal," Clouse adds. "He doesn't just sign autographs. He takes a gospel tract out of his back pocket and autographs the gospel tract. You know the guy is passionate about being a servant of Jesus Christ. That's his number one priority in what he does."[5]

Ned Jarrett has been around NASCAR for more than sixty years. The open faith of owners such as Gibbs is unlike anything that he remembers from his driving days in the 1950s and 1960s.

"It is different," Jarrett says. "I think Joe Gibbs has been a major influence on the faith that people have. I think that many people have converted because of Joe Gibbs. They see the way that he lives his life and the way that he treats people, and he's not afraid to talk about his faith."[6]

Interstate Batteries president and JGR sponsor Norm Miller has seen the fruit of Gibbs's sensitivity to the spiritual needs of those around him. During his NASCAR career, he has had a "tremendous impact" on his drivers, crew members, and their spouses, including Bobby and Donna Labonte, Terry and Kim Labonte, and Jimmy and Patti Makar.[7]

But in 2011 Gibbs's roles as a traditional executive and a spiritual leader were challenged like never before. About two months before the season started, JGR was collectively celebrating driver Kyle Busch's New Year's Eve marriage to Samantha Sarcinella. Just five months later, the mood dramatically changed following a handful of incidents, including one that took place away from the track.

On May 7 Busch got tangled up with Kevin Harvick during the Southern 500 at Darlington Speedway. Harvick felt that Busch had intentionally wrecked him late in the race, and he decided to wait for Busch on pit road. Harvick exited his car and walked over to

Busch's car. As Harvick leaned in to land a punch, Busch hit the gas and bumped Harvick's car into the pit road wall. Not surprisingly, a melee between both teams ensued as Busch attempted to escape from the car into his hauler.

Busch later claimed that he had lost reverse gear and went forward to avoid what "wasn't going to be a good situation." For his part in the incident, however, Busch was fined $25,000 and placed on probation for the next four races.[8]

About three weeks later, on May 24, Busch was cited for reckless driving and speeding when he got carried away test driving a Lexus LFA on a rural road between Mooresville and Troutman, North Carolina. He was clocked at 128 miles per hour in a zone with a forty-five-mile-per-hour limit. Later that summer, Busch received a $1,000 fine, had his license suspended for forty-five days, was ordered to log thirty hours of community service, and was placed on one year of unsupervised probation.

Things took an even more bizarre twist for Busch at the O'Reilly Auto Parts 250. After the Kansas Speedway Truck Series race, Busch gave winner Joey Coulter what he deemed to be a congratulatory bump. Coulter's team owner, Richard Childress, didn't see it that way and approached Busch about thirty minutes later, ready for a confrontation. Witnesses reported that Childress put Busch in a headlock and started punching him. NASCAR ruled that the incident did not violate Busch's probation, while Childress was fined $150,000 for his actions.

After a relatively minor incident with Elliott Sadler during the O'Reilly 200 Truck Series race at Bristol Motor Speedway on August 25, things seemed to settle down for Busch, who to that point had experienced his most tumultuous season to date. But as the season neared its end, his troubles quickly escalated to an unprecedented level.

On November 4 Busch had kicked off a rare three-race weekend at Texas Motor Speedway and the Truck Series WinStar World

Casino 350K. While running three-wide early on, Ron Hornaday slid up the track and caused Busch to hit the wall. As the caution flag came out, Busch intentionally made contact with Hornaday's rear bumper and effectively pushed him into a hard, head-on collision with the wall. It didn't help matters that Hornaday was running for the Truck Series championship. The post-race mood was additionally soured due to Kevin Harvick's involvement as Hornaday's team owner.

After the smoke cleared and the profane exchanges subsided, Busch was parked for the remaining two races and fined $50,000. It was the first time in NASCAR history that a driver had been disqualified from three races in one weekend. Busch was apologetic and even offered to sign Hornaday to a Truck Series deal for the following season. Hornaday respectfully declined after deciding to sign with Joe Denette Motorsports and remain loyal to the Chevrolet brand.

There was a great deal of speculation about Busch's future with JGR. NASCAR media members openly discussed the pros and cons of keeping him on the team. But what most people didn't realize was that Busch was dealing with some internal struggles that had led him (thanks in great part to his wife, Samantha) on a path of spiritual discovery. The newlywed couple had begun attending chapel services that year and were even reading Christian books together at home and engaging in personal times of Bible devotion.

For Norm Miller, there was never a time when letting Busch go was an option.

"We know that we're all sinners," he says. "Some [of us] are more visible than others. We saw the situation [with Kyle]. We knew that it was a flared-up deal that wasn't over just one event. It happened over a period of weeks. He just lost his temper there [in Texas]. I've done the same thing on different occasions, maybe in different ways. But we talked with him. He was repentant and sorry about it, and said he was going to do better. So we just said, 'Let's go on.'"[9]

For Miller and Gibbs, their decision was based on a desire to live by the words of Jesus in Matthew 6:14-15: "For if you forgive other people when they sin against you, your heavenly Father will also forgive you. But it you do not forgive others their sins, your Father will not forgive your sins."

In that regard, Miller wholeheartedly believes that Gibbs is the perfect owner to deal with a troubled driver.

"Joe is patient and understanding," Miller says. "He knows that Kyle's a young guy. When he started, he was younger yet. He's growing, and there's all the pressures of everything he deals with as a racer and his finances and his team and his wife. Kyle's a stallion. He's a racehorse. They're a little more temperamental than the plow horse. Through all of this, Kyle and Samantha have been growing in their faith. That's had a lot to do with their relationship with Joe and Interstate Batteries."[10]

In comparison, 2012 was a completely different year for Busch. He was by no means perfect, but he did manage to avoid many of the controversies and poor decisions from a year earlier. ESPN broadcaster Andy Petree, a former driver and team owner, recognized that Busch was making positive strides.

"I don't know the specifics, but I saw a big change in Kyle that year," Petree says. "I saw it immediately. I suspected that maybe he had been saved over the holidays. He's in church all the time, and he's different. He's definitely a different guy than he was before. He's got a lot of growing to do, but he's doing it. God is powerful. Kyle is the last guy you'd think could change, and God has changed him. It's so great to see and we'll see where it goes from here. Your walk is every day. You grow in it every day."[11]

Busch's spiritual growth has mostly been off the radar and allowed to evolve away from the scrutiny that the NASCAR platform can bring. But for Billy Mauldin, this unfinished story is evidence of what unconditional love can accomplish.

"It's amazing how God is reaching out to Kyle in such a profound way by surrounding him with these people," he says. "Those that want to have a kingdom perspective on this stuff, you see how the Lord reaches out to everybody. He might be the guy that people label the most arrogant and uncaring. But God has chosen to surround him with some phenomenally godly men. That's just an expression of God's love, not only towards Kyle, but towards all of us."[12]

Life on the Hood

Long before professional sports stadiums were selling naming rights to the highest bidders and teams were signing massive sponsorship deals, NASCAR was pioneering the advent of the moving billboard. These days, a sponsor can spend in the wide-ranging neighborhood of five to thirty-five million dollars per season in order to place logos and brand messages on a stock car.[13]

"NASCAR has always been blatantly corporate," Kyle Petty says. "Now you see the NFL, the NBA, and baseball catching up. What are they doing? They're selling their stadium rights because that's what they've got to sell. They can't put the Home Depot Dodgers on the field. If they could, by God, they would. But we can put the Coca-Cola guys on the track. We can put the Home Depot guys or the Cheerios guys on the track. That's where this sport has become a huge model for other sports and how you deal with corporate involvement."[14]

Much of what happens during the week (especially during the offseason) involves team owners jockeying for those corporate dollars and fulfilling requirements of their agreements with driver appearances, advertising campaigns, and trackside access.

For the most part, NASCAR teams promote products that maintain the sport's family-friendly approach. But sometimes, certain goods and services toe the line or even cross over into an area that causes problems for those who hold to Christian values and beliefs. Richard Petty, for instance, wouldn't put the Busch Pole Award sticker on his car, and he wouldn't participate in the Busch Clash. As an owner, Petty didn't field any cars in the Busch series until the sponsorship was replaced by Nationwide Insurance. This was mostly due to his family's aversion to promoting an alcoholic beverage.

Drivers and crew members are especially vulnerable to these owner decisions and often have no say in what logos end up on the hood of their cars and what decals get sewn onto their fire suits. Mark Martin once had the unenviable job of racing for the erectile dysfunction medication Viagra, while Kevin Conway privately struggled to justify his sponsorship deal with Extenze, a male enhancement supplement that employed adult-themed marketing strategies.

Nick Terry also dealt with the issue when he was the jack man for Kevin Harvick's #29 Budweiser car. And although the problem occasionally crossed his mind, he saw his employment with a team sponsored by an alcoholic beverage as more of an opportunity than a burden.

"I'm not bound by a shirt that I wear or whatever sponsor that represents the company," Terry says. "I'm bound to Christ. His faithfulness to save is greater than a t-shirt you wear or anything like that. So for me, it was another avenue to be able to minister and witness to people."[15]

According to Mauldin, the responses to team decisions vary from one individual to the next.

"For some, there's been a level of conviction about sponsorships," he says. "Some people have walked away from sponsorships that they felt were not representative of what they stood for, whether it was alcohol or some other things like that. You've had both scenarios play out. But unless the individual feels like God is asking them to make a public stand and walk away from that situation, you're walking away from a group of guys that are in the same situation, and they need someone to shepherd them. God can fight that battle for you."[16]

MRO chaplain Stephen Keller concurs. He too has seen drivers and crew members struggle with the sponsors they represent and wish that they didn't have certain brand names plastered all over their car or their apparel. Regardless, most ultimately side with Terry and take it in stride.

"A lot of the Christian guys out here would rather go as an instrument of light into a place of darkness," Keller says. "They'd rather help change things instead of sitting around where everything is perfect and sanitized and waiting for the world to come to them."[17]

Conversely, the rising number of outspoken Christian drivers and team owners has opened the door to interest from within the evangelical business community and Christian media community. Newmarket Films was one of the first to take advantage of this shifting paradigm. The distribution group sponsored Joe Gibbs Racing driver Bobby Labonte by advertising *The Passion of the Christ* on the hood of the #18 car at the 2004 Daytona 500.

After a lull in Christian-related sponsorships, national contemporary Christian radio network K-Love broke the ice with its sponsorship of Michael McDowell's #66 Cup car during the 2010 season. In 2011 national Christian television network Daystar sponsored Blake Koch's #81 Nationwide Series entry. That same year, Standard Publishing signed a one-race deal that placed Back2Back Ministries director Beth Guckenberger's book *Relentless Hope* on the hood of McDowell's #66 car for the Quaker State 400 at Kentucky Speedway. The move resulted in a significant spike in sales.

In April 2012 Koch was caught in a sponsorship controversy when a get-out-the-vote campaign decided to end its brief partnership with Rick Ware Racing due to ESPN's refusal to air what it deemed politically charged advertisements. Koch was later picked up by ChristianCinema.com in an effort to save his season. Koch was the beneficiary of evangelical involvement again in 2013 when Norm Miller's "I Am Second" evangelistic video series sponsored his #24 car at Daytona International Speedway's season-opening Drive4COPD 300.

"Christians are finally beginning to get it," Keller says. "Dollars and sense, there is money to be made and ministry to be advanced by having your name on a car. This is a legitimate way to have a voice heard, to get exposure. As believers, we can reach our arms out a lot further by getting behind some of these teams."[18]

The Track Gives Back

Much like a team's vital sponsorship deals, the concept of charitable giving is a constant element of NASCAR that is visible on race weekends but is orchestrated away from the track. Morgan Shepherd knows a great deal about the process as a driver, team owner, and head of the Morgan Shepherd Charitable Fund, an organization that assists the needy and physically disabled in the Virginia Mountains. It's a constant battle to garner financial support from whoever is willing to give, even if that means finding it in some unlikely places.

In 2008, at the season-ending Nationwide Series race in Homestead, Shepherd failed to qualify for the race. Afterward, he ran into Carl Edwards, who had won the race and was carrying his trophy back to the hauler.

"Don't take these moments for granted," Shepherd told Edwards. "Enjoy it. Appreciate it."[19]

As Shepherd prepared to leave, he noticed that one of Edwards's team vehicles was blocking his exit. So when he went back to ask

Edwards to have it moved, he decided to take him some brochures for his charitable organization. Edwards offered Shepherd $10,000 on the spot.

"I grabbed him and hugged him and shook his hand," Shepherd recalls. "That turned out to be a $15,000 hug, because he changed his mind and decided to give the charity $25,000 instead."[20]

It was an invaluable lesson for Shepherd, who, though disappointed to miss the race, later realized that there was a bigger plan unfolding all along.

"I had missed two races in a row, and I didn't know how I was going to get through the winter," he recalls. "I was very depressed. But when I got to my motor home and headed up the road, I was so happy, and God showed me right there what my purpose was. If I had made the race, Carl and I probably wouldn't have run across each other. Making the race would have helped me financially, but the charity wouldn't have gotten that extra $25,000."[21]

Shepherd says that his Christian faith fuels his desire to serve the needs of those who require the most help. The same is true for Patricia Driscoll, who has been president and executive director of the Armed Forces Foundation since 2001. The organization brings wounded military veterans to NASCAR races, where they not only enjoy meeting the drivers and watching the event, but also they often have their spiritual needs met by MRO representatives at the track.

"We live and breathe our troops," Driscoll says. "It's something we truly love. We want to give back to these people that have sacrificed so much for us. We as good neighbors and Christians need to pay attention to those who need our help."[22]

For Kyle Petty, the commitment to charity started when he was a driver. But the intensity of his efforts grew exponentially after he and his wife, Pattie, experienced the tragic loss of their son, Adam, during a practice run at Loudon on May 12, 2000. Prior to his death, the nineteen-year-old Adam was already engaged in charitable efforts of his own, most notably with a special-needs camp in Florida called Foggy Creek and the Starbright Foundation. He had shown interest in building a camp near the family headquarters in Level Cross, North Carolina. Adam's death sped up the process.

Richard Petty donated seventy acres of land. A family friend, Hugh Hawthorne, provided the grading work to get the land ready. And then everything fell into place. Victory Junction Gang Camp became a reality and, in essence, a tribute to the young man whose life was cut short yet was full of purpose.

"Dale Jarrett won his Man of the Year Award and donated $50,000 to the camp," Kyle Petty explains. "Then Bobby Labonte won the championship that year and donated a car to camp that we could sell and make money for the camp. The next thing you know, Tony Stewart got involved along with Kevin Harvick, Jeff Gordon, Jimmie Johnson, Dale Earnhardt, Ryan Newman, the Busch brothers, and many others. Michael Waltrip even ran a marathon as a fundraiser for the camp."[23]

At any given moment, Kyle Petty can pull a wad of checks and cash out of his pocket from fans who randomly walk up to him at tracks across the country. While the initial investment was just under thirty million dollars, the facility (which is free to all the campers) costs in the neighborhood of three million dollars a year to operate. Victory Junction Gang Camp welcomes well over one thousand kids representing twelve to fourteen different disease groups each year, including spina bifida, hemophilia, juvenile rheumatoid arthritis, AIDS, cancer, leukemia, heart disease, and asthma.[24]

When asked where Kyle's giving heart comes from, father Richard Petty quickly points to his son's mother, Lynda.

"She always had something going at the church or at the school," he explains. "She worked for the PTA. She was a Scout teacher. She was in 4H. Kyle grew up in it. He was able to get out and see how lucky we were to have the advantages in life. We worked for it, but we could go, and we could do, and we were all healthy. So when he goes out and he sees all of these other people, he wants to give back."25

Kyle Petty agrees with his father's assessment but pays additional homage to the faith-driven efforts of his grandmother Petty and his grandmother Owens, both of whom were committed servants in their respective Methodist churches.

"They were always doing something," he says. "We grew up in small communities and the churches are the hearts of small communities. When somebody's house burns down, the church is the first one there to try to do something. The church has the covered-dish suppers to raise money for a family who's lost something or had a tragedy. That's faith in action."26

Mark Martin is another driver who has made contributions to Victory Junction Gang Camp. He has visited the camp, made appearances to raise awareness, and participated in fundraisers.

"Richard's the King," Martin says. "That pretty much sums that up. But Kyle, in my opinion, is the man of the century. He really is a great man. Richard should be so proud to have a son like that. The camp is an incredible undertaking, and [the Petty family have] been victors in that. Like I said, Kyle Petty is, in my opinion, man of the century."27

NASCAR's giving spirit has been passed down from each generation to the next, and it doesn't appear to be tapering off anytime soon, thanks to a collection of young Christian drivers who have made serving others the centerpiece of their faith journey. Trevor Bayne, Ricky Stenhouse Jr., Michael McDowell, and Justin Allgaier are among those who have traveled to Mexico in support of Back2Back Ministries' orphanage there.

Their actions have also made an impact on other star drivers, such as Carl Edwards, who has never made a public profession of faith but clearly has been moved to action. Though not highly publicized, Edwards gives all of his trophies away to mentally or physically disabled fans. He has also quietly visited Lonnie Clouse in Monterrey.

"He could have had all kinds of media following him," Clouse says. "He had just come in second place for the Cup championship. He could have had all kinds of opportunities to exploit that, but he chose to come down here and be a part of what was going on: to raise awareness and love on these orphans."[28]

At the 2010 Nationwide Series race at Road America, the drivers were shown a Harley Davidson motorcycle that would be given to the race winner. It gave Edwards an idea.

"I knew that if I won the race, that motorcycle would be mine," he says. "So, I was talking to my friend Lonnie about selling the bike if I won and giving the proceeds to his orphanage."[29]

Edwards proceeded to win the race, and he immediately set into motion an online auction that gave fans a chance to bid on his new motorcycle along with other pieces of race memorabilia.

Clouse is thankful not only for these drivers' efforts, but also for the selfless nature of their giving.

"They don't do it for the public acknowledgment," he says. "It's neat to see how humble [they] are and how they don't want to do anything for the accolades of the world. They just want to do things unnoticed. They're doing it out of a good heart. They just want to do what's right."[30]

NOTES

1. Nick Terry, interview with the author, October 8, 2011.
2. Ibid.
3. Blake Koch, interview with the author, October 8, 2011.
4. Lonnie Clouse, interview with the author, August 21, 2012.
5. Ibid.
6. Ned Jarrett, interview with the author, August 21, 2012.
7. Norm Miller, interview with the author, August 21, 2012.
8. Jeff Gluck, "Kevin Harvick, Kyle Busch Clash after Southern 500 at Darlington Raceway," SBNation, May 8, 2011.

(http://www.sbnation.com/nascar/2011/5/8/2160051/kevin-harvick-kyle-busch-darlington-raceway-southern-500-nascar-2011).

9. Norm Miller, interview with the author, August 21, 2012.
10. Ibid.
11. Andy Petree, interview with the author, October 5, 2012.
12. Billy Mauldin, interview with the author, December 5, 2011.
13. Robert Klara, "Your Brand Here: Ever Wonder What It Costs to Get a Sticker on a NASCAR Car?" Adweek, January 28, 2013 (http://www.adweek.com/news/advertising-branding/your-brand-here-146795).
14. Kyle Petty, interview with the author, October 7, 2005.
15. Nick Terry, interview with the author, October 8, 2011.
16. Billy Mauldin, interview with the author, December 5, 2011.
17. Stephen Keller, interview with the author, October 9, 2011.
18. Ibid.
19. Morgan Shepherd, interview with the author, November 5, 2009.
20. Ibid.
21. Ibid.
22. Patricia Driscoll, interview with the author, September 29, 2012.
23. Kyle Petty, interview with the author, October 7, 2005.
24. Ibid.
25. Richard Petty, interview with the author, October 7, 2005.
26. Kyle Petty, interview with the author, October 7, 2005.
27. Mark Martin, interview with the author, October 28, 2008.
28. Lonnie Clouse, interview with the author, August 21, 2012.
29. "NASCAR Driver Carl Edwards and Copart Team Up to Auction Edwards' Harley Davidson Motorcycle and Race Memorabilia to Benefit Back2Back Ministries' Orphan Care Program," Back2Back Ministries, October 2010 (http://back2back.org/2010/10/carledwardsnascarauction/).
30. Lonnie Clouse, interview with the author, August 21, 2012.

CHAPTER 12

"Jesus, Take the Wheel"

There's nothing unusual about a stock car journalist or broadcast reporter being asked to wait for an interview subject. Cup drivers such as Jeff Gordon, Jimmie Johnson, Greg Biffle, and Danica Patrick can easily get sidetracked with sponsor appearances, autograph requests, charity functions, and team meetings. Even drivers from the Nationwide and Craftsman Truck series, rising stars such as Austin Dillon, Ty Dillon, and Kyle Larson, stay busy fielding an array of media and fan-related obligations.

They don't come around much, but when they do, writers looking for an interview with Morgan Shepherd might be surprised to find that he's quite a busy guy too. They might even be asked to wait a few minutes before NASCAR's elder statesman can show up for the appointment. And there's a pretty good chance that Shepherd could get pulled away briefly in the middle of the conversation.

But the seventy-something racing legend's hectic schedule looks nothing like the workload of his fellow competitors. Since Shepherd parted ways with Victory Motorsports, a team that he cofounded with a group of Christian businessmen, and set up his own race team during the summer of 2006, Shepherd's #89 car has been mostly unsponsored—that is, if you don't include the self-funded entity Faith Motorsports. And at first glance, if you didn't know better, you might assume that Jesus himself was the team's sponsor. It's hard to miss the bright green (or sometimes red) body with yellow numbers and oval-encased logo on the hood that says "Racing With Jesus," the word "Jesus" in large red lettering and a blue cross in the background. On the rear panel, another slogan, "Racing For Souls," is equally visible.

Compared to most cars, Shepherd's ride is practically naked outside of a select few stickers that reference NASCAR's Nationwide series, official fuel provider Sunoco, and the ubiquitous Chevrolet manufacturer's symbol. Without the massive sponsor demands and, quite frankly, with a less-than-fanatical fan base hovering around his hauler seeking autographs or hoping for a quick glimpse and photo-op of their favorite driver, Shepherd instead deals with racing-related tasks that few other drivers think twice about.

Mostly, this means that Shepherd can be found underneath the hood of his own car showing the young, less-experienced crew members a trick or two about horsepower, handling, or suspension.

"My life has been self-taught education," Shepherd says. "I can hardly work a VCR, but I can take a pile of metal and build a race car out of it. I can build engines. I can build chassis. That was all self-taught. I was rebuilding engines in high school. Today's kids are computer nuts. They're doing the computers and the cell phones. They're texting each other. I mean, I have no idea how to text somebody. We're in the same world, but the technology has changed everything so much."[1]

Last of the Moonshiners

Shepherd has come a long way since his days in the hills of western North Carolina, where his parents were farm workers. His father, Jesse Clay Shepherd, also worked in the logging industry and more than dabbled in the illegal but then-popular moonshine business. After serving a year in prison, Shepherd's father did his best to walk the straight and narrow, but the allure of good money was too difficult to resist.

"It was a way of life back where we came from," Shepherd says about his father. "There weren't a lot of jobs in Ferguson. My dad made a living with logging. He had a couple mules and an old truck, and then he made moonshine on the side. The first time I really remember my dad was when I was somewhere around four and a half years old. I saw this bus pull up across the creek. My mom said, 'That's your dad coming home.' He'd been in prison for a year for making moonshine. Back in the '40s and '50s, that was sort of the way of life for people up in the mountains."[2]

Even Shepherd briefly fell into the moonshine trap. In his late teens, he and his friend Clifford Baker built a still in Shepherd's basement. One night, when they headed home from work, less than a mile away, they heard a loud explosion. The local Alcoholic Beverage Control (ABC) agents, or "revenuers," part of the U.S. Treasury Department responsible for enforcing bootlegging laws, had discovered the still and unceremoniously blown it to bits.[3]

But that close call didn't deter the wayward youths from their entrepreneurial endeavors. Shepherd and his buddy knew where to buy "white liquor" for their scaled-back distribution. On one fateful day, the duo went to nearby Hildebrand to pick some up, but it wasn't ready, and the seller told them to come back in an hour.

"We noticed something wasn't quite right," Shepherd recalls. "We saw these maroon Buicks and all these cops along the way. We were coming back down [route] 6470, and right after you pass Hickory Speedway and pass Steve White's dealership, there's no turnoffs between there and all the way into Conover. They waited 'til we got past where we couldn't turn off or really run from them."[4]

Then, seemingly out of nowhere, a host of police cars and ABC vehicles converged upon the startled travelers. Shepherd estimates between eighteen and twenty cars carrying police officers from Conover and Hickory, plus several "ABC men," quickly closed in on Clifford Baker's 1959 Pontiac Catalina.

"We didn't have a load of liquor, but happened to have a Pepsi-Cola bottle sitting on the seat, and it was full of it," Shepherd says. "I told Clifford, 'Pull off on the grass. I'm gonna knock off the top of this Pepsi bottle. Just keep going until I get this thing emptied.' So I eased the door open and we kept driving in the grass and I got it emptied and let go of it."[5]

Fortunately for Shepherd and Baker, the authorities were so focused on the car and its driver that they didn't notice Shepherd pouring out the illegal substance.

"They just knew they had us," he says. "They told us to get out of the car. They were knocking on the panels. They were in the trunk. They were up under the gas tank. They just knew they had us. But we got rid of the last little bit, and they let us go. That was the last time we ever hauled any moonshine."[6]

His father's dubious past and his own experiences as a moonshine runner make Shepherd the only active NASCAR driver with direct ties to stock car racing's inconvenient history. Thankfully for Shepherd, he had long since realized the need for a sustainable skill. Much earlier in life he had taken a liking to mechanics. At the age of ten, he took apart his Whizzer bike, a popular motorcycle brand that was first produced in 1939, and reassembled the parts every week. Sometimes he would add new parts that he picked up at the Western Auto store.[7]

His bike played an important role in the purchase of his first car. Just twelve years old at the time, Shepherd gave a man twelve dollars, his Whizzer, two flying squirrels, a grey squirrel, and a twenty-gauge shotgun in exchange for a 1937 Chevrolet Coach.

"I did the same thing with it," Shepherd says. "I'd take it apart and put it together. That's how I learned to be a mechanic. Before I turned thirteen, I was able to rebuild engines. I rebuilt engines for high school boys. So I was sort of self-taught over the years. That's how I got into racing."[8]

Shepherd's racing career could have started much earlier, but he kept getting into trouble with the law for racing the back roads. His reputation precluded him from getting his driver's license until he was twenty-six years old. So for ten years, Shepherd lived vicariously through the drivers at some nearby racetracks.[9]

In 1967 Shepherd got his first shot behind the wheel at Hickory Motor Speedway driving Late Models. Two years later, he had a breakout season driving a 1955 Chevy in the Hobby Division. Shepherd won twenty-one of twenty-nine races that year, and he owes much of his success to close friends such as Glen Canipe, people who gave him a few bucks at a time or donated car parts to help him along.[10]

Shepherd, who has held his NASCAR license since that first racing season in 1967, didn't get his first Cup (then sponsored by Winston) start until 1970, when he finished nineteenth out of twenty-two cars at Hickory Motor Speedway driving the #93 Chevrolet for owner Alan Flowers. Shepherd quickly reminds people that he has "raced longer than Richard Petty."[11] He would never, however, compare himself to the Hall of Fame legend. Shepherd respects NASCAR's history too much to even attempt to overstate his contributions to stock car racing.

"I believe I'm in the greatest sport in the world," Shepherd says. "There's no other sport that's such a family sport where we care about others, whether it's the drivers of the past like [Neil] Castle or the Wood brothers. We're all one big family. Even with the young kids that are coming in today, the majority of them still recognize where the sport comes from and where it's going."[12]

Shepherd might not have the racing legacy of Richard Petty, Dale Earnhardt, Darrell Waltrip, or Dale Jarrett, but he has made a significant impact on the sport. After some poor life decisions derailed his career in the early 1970s, he had a lengthy run in the

Cup series from 1977 to 2006 with brief interruptions during the 1979–1980 and 2000–2001 seasons, and he picked up top-ten finishes in about half of his starts, as well as four outright wins. Shepherd also ran fifty-five races in the Truck Series between 1997 and 2008, in addition to a lengthy career in the Nationwide Series (previously known as the Busch Series through the 2007 season), where he is still active today. There, he has fifteen career wins in more than 350 career starts.[13]

Late in the 2010 season, Shepherd had held his own driving the #89 Racing With Jesus car and caught the attention of Richard Childress, who then asked the veteran driver to take the wheel of his #21 car. Although unsponsored throughout that run, Childress allowed Shepherd to put his "Jesus" logo on the car at the Kansas race and beyond, a practice that he started in 2001 with the now-defunct Victory in Jesus Racing. With Johnny Chapman or Brett Rowe driving the #89 for Shepherd, at times there were two "Jesus" cars simultaneously on the track.

While being asked to drive for one of the sport's great owners at the age of sixty-eight is certainly something worthy of boasting, Shepherd goes back to 1985 for his career highlight. That's when he earned his second career Cup win driving in Jack Beebe's #47 Buick. Five years later, racing for Bud Moore Engineering in the #15 Motorcraft Ford Thunderbird, Shepherd recorded his career-high Cup points finish in fifth place along with his third career win at the season-ending Atlanta Journal 500. During the 1993 season, he made history in Atlanta when he became the second-oldest driver to win a Cup race, at the age of fifty-one years, five months, and eight days, roughly a year younger than Harry Gant, who had become the oldest Cup winner a year earlier.[14]

Shepherd continued to flirt with idea of racing on a regular basis in the Cup series up until 2006. But with the advent of NASCAR's Car of Tomorrow, the fifth generation of car used in the Cup series, and the increased expenses involved, the writing was on the wall.

Since then, he has focused exclusively on the Nationwide Series, in part due to his genuine love of the sport—a fact that hasn't gone unnoticed throughout the garage.

"What inspires us [about Shepherd] is that he's so dedicated to what he's doing," Cup superstar Tony Stewart says. "He spends every dime he has to come out and support NASCAR and support the Nationwide Series. A lot of times he's his own crew chief, and his family is part of his crew. He's learned to do a lot with very little."[15]

While driving in the Truck Series, Shepherd proved Stewart's last statement to be true while reflecting his vast knowledge of stock car racing. His inspiration came from former driver Wendell Scott, the first black driver to win a Cup race. Shepherd recalled stories about how Scott, a pioneer of diversity in the sport during the 1960s and early 1970s, would get out of his car during pit stops and refuel his own car and change his tires. He would even take time to drink some Pepsi and eat some cheese crackers before climbing back in and heading back onto the track.

Shepherd had done everything in racing up to that point. He had driven, engineered, and administrated, but he never did a pit stop like Wendell Scott did—until, that is, the 2001 Truck race in Kentucky.

"The NASCAR official just stood there and was amazed at what was going on," Shepherd recalls. "I got out of the car and changed my tires. Then I got me a Pepsi and some cheese crackers and took a drink and a couple bites and jumped back in the car and drove away. That NASCAR official was just looking at me like I was crazy."[16]

NASCAR has since written a rule that disallows drivers from getting out of the car to change their own tires. Some insiders actually refer to it as "The Morgan Shepherd Rule." But Shepherd is just tickled that he tried it once.

"Now I can say I've done it all," he says with a huge grin.

"He Can Still Race"

Perhaps it's that cavalier attitude that has endeared Shepherd to drivers, crews, owners, and NASCAR officials alike. The fact that the old man can still drive doesn't hurt.

"Morgan's been out here a long, long time," former Motor Racing Outreach chaplain Tim Griffin says. "Back in the day when he was in his prime, he was a legend. He was very respected, and he still is respected. He's an old-school guy, and he'll always be an old-school guy. You have to respect a fellow who is at that stage in his career and continues to come out here and compete. He can still race."[17]

Nationwide Series regular Eric McClure jokes about how seeing Shepherd in his rearview mirror usually means there's a good chance he's about to get passed.[18] Shepherd also receives personal praise on a regular basis from Cup drivers such as Carl Edwards and big-time owners such as Roger Penske and Chip Ganassi, "people that I didn't think were paying any attention to what we're doing," he notes.[19]

Shepherd claims that healthy choices and exercise, which consists primarily of roller-skating, help him stay in good shape.

"Carl Edwards can do the backflip, but I bet he can't roller skate like I can," Shepherd quips. "I can really take the heat good. I try to stay in shape with my roller-skating and other exercising I do. When these other guys are playing with their computers, I'm roller skating or working on the racecar. So I've got them whipped already on the physical end of it."[20]

And then there's the spiritual component of his life, which Shepherd credits for most for his longevity in the rough-and-tumble sport.

Shepherd admits that he never imagined that he would be racing at the age of seventy. "I've watched drivers quit in their late thirties. Ned Jarrett quit in his thirties. But I still have this great passion and love for this sport, and undoubtedly, the Lord wants me to be here because I wouldn't be able to be here and do it. I don't run out of gas when it comes to running the miles. I can withstand the heat better than anybody out there. God has kept me tough."[21]

Hard Racing, Harder Living

Shepherd wasn't always cognizant of good decision-making. When first breaking into the NASCAR scene during the late 1960s, he soon discovered that hard racing on the track had led to an even harder lifestyle outside his car. Shepherd holds Bible studies every Tuesday at his race shop in Conover, North Carolina, and sometimes he has to convince attendees that he used to be a very different kind of person. It's hard for them to imagine that their straight-laced, Jesus-loving leader could have once led such a rough existence.

"I only cared about Morgan Shepherd," he says. "I partied and drank. Whatever I could do for Morgan Shepherd, that's what I did. That's what the average person does when they don't know Christ."[22]

At the age of twenty-nine, Shepherd was heading for the top with a bullet, but the young man with the sketchy past was quickly drawn back into a cycle of heavy drinking and reckless womanizing. Although married at the time, Shepherd would often disappear for several days after alcoholic binges. He knew that he had a problem, and he even stopped drinking for a year, but ultimately the temptation was too great. The alcohol abuse severely hampered his career, and even worse, it destroyed his marriage. When he returned from Daytona in 1975, Shepherd took the biggest blow when he found that his wife had left him.

"God let me get to the lowest point in my life on February 23, 1975," he says. "I finally fell to my knees. I had said the words before, but this time I was serious because I was one miserable human being. When I received Christ, he made me see all of the good men in prison that wouldn't be there had they not taken that drink, and all the families and all the things that were wasted and down the drain. I've never been tempted by that ever since."[23]

Shepherd was so serious about his commitment that in 1982 he turned down a major sponsorship deal from the Coors Brewing Company. There was no way he could allow himself to be attached, even just commercially, to the substance that had cost him so dearly. Then in 1999 a $25 million, multiyear sponsorship deal with some South Carolina insurance agencies fell through, leaving Shepherd with insurmountable debt. The wealth that he had attained throughout the 1980s and 1990s was virtually gone.[24]

Through it all, Shepherd has always relied first and foremost in his Christian faith. And that's what continues to drive his efforts in NASCAR and with the Morgan Shepherd Foundation, his charity outfit that has been operational since 1986.

"We take a stand for Jesus Christ, our Lord and Savior," Shepherd says. "When the trailer goes down the road, somebody's got to read those words [Racing With Jesus]. I'm sure there are people that don't like it. But the majority of our country supports what we're doing."[25]

"Jesus, Take the Wheel"

Many of NASCAR's much younger Christian drivers have taken notice of Shepherd's outward expressions of faith. It's fairly common to see him sitting on the front row at the Nationwide chapel service each week, while drivers such as Trevor Bayne and Justin Allgaier follow his example, sitting nearby.

"He probably would have quit ten or fifteen years ago if 'Racing With Jesus' had not been on the car," Allgaier believes. "He feels like that's a good way to get the message out. Racetracks are places where people tend to come to lose their inhibitions a little bit and let loose and relax. It's probably not always a good thing. So for him, it's a good way to get people to just think. Most people don't think about [God] until they see something or they hear something. And then they think, 'Wait, maybe this isn't the right way to do it.'"[26]

Shepherd is also making an impact on drivers who have never made a public declaration of faith. During the 2008 season, when Shepherd was struggling to keep the #89 car afloat, Kevin Harvick donated a Nationwide car to help keep him running. Retired Christian driver Dale Jarrett committed to buy his tires for the spring Charlotte race. And then Tony Stewart took it a step further by committing to buy Shepherd's tires for a full season—a commitment that continued well beyond that year.

"It was a situation where Kevin [Harvick] and myself saw the effort he was making and wanted to help him," Stewart says. "It grew to be a little larger than what I anticipated doing actually, but it's hard not to fall in love with Morgan and what he's doing."[27]

Even though things had improved enough by the 2010 season for full seasons of operation, Shepherd was still operating at a deficit. He points at the 2011 race in Chicago as a prime example. After getting blown away down the straightaway by the other drivers, he took his car to Johnny Davis's shop for a comparison. Shepherd's engine had thirty-four less units of horsepower than Davis's, and Davis's cars had roughly thirty less units of horsepower than the series' top teams.[28] Despite those difficult obstacles, Shepherd never ceases to be amazed at how his race team's needs are met more often than not.

"It seems like somebody comes along and helps keep us here," he says. "When all of this happened with Kevin and Tony, I'd be riding down the road, and tears would just about come to my eyes. Why would these two guys help Morgan Shepherd? What would cause them to do this? I just believe it's a God thing. God's working on them."[29]

Heading into the 2013 season, NASCAR reduced the Nationwide field from forty-three cars to forty cars, making it that much more difficult for Shepherd to qualify from week to week. That didn't stop him from making history by becoming the oldest driver to start a Cup Series race. At the age of 71, he bested the previous record held by Jim Fitzgerald who was 65 when he raced during the 1987 season. In his first Cup start since 2006, Shepherd set the new mark in New Hampshire at the Camping World RV Sales 301 while driving for Brian Keselowski Motorsports.

But as far as the seasoned veteran is concerned, his NASCAR existence is proof positive that miracles do happen. How else do you explain a driver in his seventies still hanging around a young person's sport? For what other reason can the son of a moonshiner still find a place in NASCAR? Shepherd is understandably confident in his answer to those questions.

"We take a little bit and can still qualify in races against guys who've got millions of dollars," Shepherd says. "God has blessed me at my age with talent and blessed me with the opportunity. And it's all so I can carry the name of Jesus and try to influence people to better their lives."[30]

NOTES
1. Morgan Shepherd, interview with the author, November 5, 2009.
2. Morgan Shepherd, interview with the author, October 5, 2011.
3. Ibid.
4. Ibid.
5. Ibid.
6. Ibid.
7. Ibid.
8. Ibid.
9. Alan Middleton, "The Last of the Moonshiners: Morgan Shepherd Labors to Maintain a Link between Racing and Its Notorious Roots," *Stock Car Racing*, February 2009.
10. Ibid.
11. Morgan Shepherd, interview with the author, November 5, 2009.
12. Ibid.

13. NASCAR.com (http://www.nascar.com/en_us/nationwide-series/stats/driver-stats/morgan-shepherd.html).

14. Morgan Shepherd, interview with the author, November 5, 2009.

15. Tony Stewart, response to question by the author during press conference at the Dickies 500 in Fort Worth, Texas, November 5, 2009.

16. Morgan Shepherd, interview with the author, November 5, 2009.

17. Tim Griffin, interview with the author, November 6, 2009.

18. Eric McClure, interview with the author, November 6, 2009.

19. Morgan Shepherd, interview with the author, November 5, 2009.

20. Ibid.

21. Morgan Shepherd, interview with the author, October 5, 2011.

22. Morgan Shepherd, interview with the author, November 5, 2009.

23. Ibid.

24. Middleton, "The Last of the Moonshiners."

25. Morgan Shepherd, interview with the author, November 5, 2009.

26. Justin Allgaier, interview with the author, November 6, 2009.

27. Tony Stewart, response to question by the author during press conference at the Dickies 500 in Fort Worth, Texas, November 5, 2009.

28. Morgan Shepherd, interview with the author, October 5, 2011.

29. Morgan Shepherd, interview with the author, November 5, 2009.

30. Ibid.

CHAPTER 13

Mortal Men...and Women

From the average NASCAR fan's perspective, the pavement might seem smoother on the other side of the catch fence. Drivers get paid large sums of money to drive fast cars. They always seem so happy standing next to their spouses and children during the pre-race ceremonies. They travel the country to do special appearances and hobnob with celebrities from across the entertainment spectrum.

What's not to love about the NASCAR lifestyle?

If you had asked Darrell Waltrip that question about thirty years ago, he probably would have had a largely positive response. After all, during his heyday, there was everything to love about being a world-class stock car driver.

But over time, Waltrip learned a few things about real life. He suffered through some disappointments. He had some close calls on the track. He began to deal with many of the same personal issues that all people experience. As it turned out, the NASCAR lifestyle was still great, but far from perfect.

"People get hurt in this sport," Waltrip says. "People get killed. People have marital problems. People have financial problems. People have the same difficulties as anyone else out there."[1]

In his six years as a Motor Racing Outreach (MRO) chaplain, Dale Beaver had a pretty good idea of what was going on in the lives of his constituency. He knew many of the drivers, crew chiefs, crew members, NASCAR officials, and their families well enough to gauge when things were going well and when things weren't going so great.

"Most of the time when someone was at chapel that wasn't normally there, I knew the catalyst that got them there," Beaver says. "That's why I was constantly trying to make sure I was connecting the Scripture to something that was relevant to their lives. The attention span of that bunch is not very long at all."[2]

Risky Business

NASCAR drivers, at least the ones who last very long in the sport, tend to have the ability to tuck bad moments on the track deep into the recesses of their memory. It might be a poor decision that costs them a top-five finish or, even worse, causes them to wreck their car. A lot of times, it's something that wasn't even their fault, but rather the result of a fellow competitor's indiscretion. That's when that internal filter comes in handy and allows them to get back out there with minimal fear of a repeat episode.

"I only ask myself hard questions outside of the car," Sam Hornish Jr. says. "I try not to be thinking about them inside the car. When you start having a lot of those thoughts inside the car, you should probably get out of the car."[3]

On April 4, 2008, at Texas Motor Speedway, Michael McDowell had one of those bad moments that he'd like to forget about. In just his second Cup race, he was qualifying for Michael Waltrip Racing (MWR) in the #00 car. Just before McDowell's run, David Reutimann blew his engine, which left a sizable oil spill. The NASCAR officials scrambled to clean up the mess with a substance called "SpeedyDry." McDowell waited on pit road for twenty minutes before he was given the signal to proceed.

"On my second lap, I got up in [the SpeedyDry], and the car got loose," McDowell says. "We'd actually pulled the brakes back just to have more speed, which in hindsight was probably a bad decision. I went to the brake and nothing was there, so I went to the other pedal, which is the gas and turned to the right and the thing just took off and shot up the racetrack. As I was going up the racetrack, I knew it was going to be a very big impact."[4]

After hitting the wall at an estimated 170 miles per hour, McDowell's car caught fire and barrel rolled eight times down the track as the stunned crowd looked on.

"As it was rolling, everything slowed down," he explains. "It just got real still. It felt like it wasn't going to stop. It just kept rolling and rolling and rolling. I didn't know if I'd made it over the fence and I was on the other side of the racetrack. I didn't know if I was going to land on a motor home in the infield because it felt like it took two or three minutes to stop."[5]

When McDowell's car finally stopped on the apron, it had, amazingly, landed on its wheels. After catching his breath, he lowered the window net and emerged relatively unscathed.

"A lot of credit goes to the safety measures in the new car," McDowell says. "But I tell everyone that when you look at the wreck and you look at the car, it wasn't the day that God chose for me to die. That's really how I look at it."[6]

Jami McDowell is happy to concur with her husband's assessment. As she watched the wreck unfold on the big screen from pit lane, her stomach dropped, and her heart skipped a few beats. It helped that Michael was able to get out of his car so quickly.

"Michael's PR representative was standing there with me, and she did not give me a moment to panic," she says. "She took me to the medical center right away. I really had no time to let panic set in. It honestly didn't impact me until afterwards, when I had to watch the crash over and over again on TV. I got to the point where I didn't want to see it anymore."[7]

When Jami arrived at the medical center, MRO chaplains Tim Griffin and Lonnie Clouse were already there. Seeing those familiar faces provided her some much-needed comfort and peace. But most importantly, Jami says, she is glad that she had forged a relationship with God four years earlier.

"Many people ask me how I do this with my husband going around the track two hundred miles an hour every weekend, and how I let him back in the car after an accident like that," she says. "But this is our life, and this is his dream. Having faith in the Lord has made it easier for me. I know that every day [Michael] has on earth is because God wants him to be here. When God's ready to take him home, he'll take him home. So there's no need to worry about anything. Whether he's in the car or driving the motor home or doing a project at home, God is going to choose when [to take] him home. I really cling to that and know that none of my anxiety or worry is going to give him an extra hour of life. I was definitely thankful after the Texas crash, and I do believe it was a miracle and that God saved him. I believe that [Michael] is here on this earth for a reason."[8]

Ashley Allgaier hasn't gone through quite the same experience as her good friend Jami McDowell, but she has seen her husband, Justin, get banged up on the track more than his fair share. She tends to get nervous only when he's racing at Daytona and Talladega, but it was his first Nationwide Series race at Charlotte in 2008 that gave her the biggest scare.

"When he wrecked, his car went up in flames," Allgaier says. "He didn't get out of the car right away. It was his first race with Penske, and there were all kinds of emotions. I had no clue where the infield care center was, and I practically got lost trying to get there. By the time I got there, he was checked out of the doctor's [room] and looking for me."[9]

In subsequent incidents, Allgaier has also been thankful that MRO chaplains are on site during those moments of uncertainty.

"Sometimes you just need that friendly face to calm you down," she says. "That's what they can provide for us. If we need a prayer or whatever, they're there to give us whatever we need. It could be a bottle of water or a hand to hold. They never ask questions. They just provide."[10]

Michael McDowell's wreck and other scary moments like it provide meaningful wake-up calls not just for NASCAR's safety team, but also for the drivers, who put themselves in harm's way. Matt Kenseth believes that while it can be easy to get complacent with the high-tech advances that have been developed since the rash of fatalities in 2000 and 2001, there are some things that simply can't be predicted.

"I believe that when it's your day [to go], it's your day [to go]," he says. "God's more in control than we are. Obviously, you still take all the precautions and safety measures inside your car. But you can't help think about it sometimes, and that you could be next if you make a mistake."[11]

And as far as Waltrip is concerned, that should still be a sobering thought for anyone who gets behind the wheel of a NASCAR racing machine.

"This is a dangerous sport," Waltrip adds. "If you're going to have a relationship and walk pretty close to the Lord, this is a pretty good sport to do it in. Up until the last few years, the chances were a lot greater that you could get killed doing this. I've had a lot of people tell me, 'I'm just not ready to give it up. I'm not ready to do that yet. I'll [accept Christ] when the time comes.' I always think of a couple of examples, and Dale Earnhardt is one of them. Do you think in a blink of an eye he had time to say, 'Lord, forgive me'? At 180 miles an hour, he wasn't thinking about that. I think everybody in this business knows that you need to keep your house in order because you never know who's going to knock on the door."[12]

Job Insecurity

One of the biggest fears that most drivers and team members face starts on the track and ends in the boardroom. Poor or even mediocre performance can be just as disastrous as a nasty on-track incident. There are no guarantees that a job will be there at the end of the season, and in fact, it can be taken away after any given race.

Perhaps that's why McDowell's first thoughts as he sat in his just-wrecked car that day in 2008 weren't related to physical health.

"Man, I hope I don't get fired or lose my ride," he recalls thinking. He explains, "In motorsports, you'll hear a lot of people say, 'That guy was really good until he had that big wreck' or 'He was on his way, but then he had that accident.' I didn't want to be that guy. I knew I had to get right back in it."[13]

His wife admits falling prey to the same mindset.

"I've been around this for so long that the competitiveness has rubbed off on me," Jami says. "When he's in a crash now, I'm thinking, 'Is the car okay? Can we get back out on the track?'"[14]

As a driver, turned crew member, turned crew chief, turned car owner, Andy Petree spent nearly twenty years getting caught up in NASCAR's daily grind, although at times he did not truly understand the toll that it was taking on all aspects of his existence.

"I've been a Christian my whole life," Petree says. "I was raised in church. But you get in that garage area, and you get so focused on these goals. It really pulls you away from church. We had MRO, and it was a big part of our life, and I thank God for them. But that lifestyle is so hard. You're trying to beat people, and you have this attitude that they're trying to take something from you. It's a dog-eat-dog world in there, and it's just not healthy for a good Christian life."[15]

Petree calls the time that he took away from the sport "the best two years" of his life. He eventually returned to a much more manageable role as an ESPN analyst.[16]

According to Dale Beaver, what Petree and others like him needed then and continue to need now is "help experiencing life outside of racing."

"That's critical to their walk with Christ," he says. "Yes, you can grow as a believer in the context of competition, as difficult as it may be. But I've got to get you out of here visiting some hospitals and visiting some sick people every now and then. We've got to get back in Charlotte sometimes, and we've got to be a part of something that's outside of racing—something that's not just an appearance or a promotional gig."[17]

Dr. Jerry Punch might have one of the more unique perspectives on the challenges that come with the NASCAR lifestyle. He has experienced many harrowing moments as an emergency room doctor, and yet at times it seems that his work as a pit road reporter can be just as physically, emotionally, and spiritually challenging.

"I remember one night in particular, I had done a Thursday night football game somewhere on the West Coast," Punch says. "I red-eyed all night to get to Darlington on Friday, and I hosted qualifying on ESPN. That night, I went to my hotel, and I was exhausted. I hadn't been to sleep. I did notes on the plane all the way over. Now, I had to prepare to do what was then the Busch [Series] race the next day. I was sitting in my room with a cup of coffee, and I was trying to stay awake at nine o'clock on a Friday night. I called my wife and said, 'I don't know if I'm going to make it. I'm doing the best I can.' And she said, 'You just put what happens tomorrow in God's hands. Close your books. Close your notes. Put them away, and go to bed. Just have faith that what needs to happen will happen.' There was an incredible peace in that."[18]

Men like Petree and Punch may have figured out that the source of their strength rests in God's hands, not their own. But according to Billy Mauldin, there are still many profound opportunities for ministry to those dealing with career uncertainties, marital and family problems, and separation from the outside world, a common occurrence that he deems "the most devastating human pull" in the sport.

"The sport can separate you from family," Mauldin says. "Young guys can be separated from parents. Married folks can be separated from spouses. When you first start out and you're gone for the weekends, it's hard being gone for a while, then you make some lifestyle adjustments. Your family adjusts. You adjust. You accept it. But if that separation isn't watched real carefully, it can begin to create a distance between you and the other people that are there to be your support base and your encouragement. Eventually you find yourself out on an island. That's when things begin to get messed up. It's a slow, gradual process. Then all of a sudden two married people aren't sure if they love each other anymore. But it's really just the separation. Then it becomes a lot easier to stay away. You begin to justify an affair or the idea that you're not going to be involved in your kid's life anymore, so why try?"[19]

That's why Sam Hornish Jr. believes that MRO's presence, while necessary for those times when people are shaken by harrowing moments on the track, is even more vital when it comes to troubling issues that individuals within the community often face.

"The best times for MRO to be there are when people are just going through things that the rest of us have no idea about, like when things aren't going well at home," he says. "The greater good of having MRO there is for people to have someone to talk to about their problems. The chaplains get to know them, and then they're able to invite them to chapel. A lot of those people will go to chapel, and they'll start to have thoughts they haven't had before. It brings them to God in a way that probably would have never happened if MRO wasn't there."[20]

Double-Edged Swords

The concept of mortality is most often associated with death. But in reality, it has everything to do with the flawed nature of humanity. Humanity is imperfect. Human beings are fallible. Humanity is finite. Sometimes our heroes can seem to have superhuman qualities, but they are subject to the laws of nature just like the rest of us.

When professional athletes choose to follow Christ, it can be easy for fellow Christians to attach high expectations that are, quite frankly, unattainable, and that usually set the high-profile individuals up for failure. NASCAR drivers are no less susceptible to that reality, but according to Darrell Waltrip, problems don't tend to be as magnified as in other professional sports.

"We keep it to a minimum here," he says. "Guys don't screw up very often. It's part of our upbringing. It's because of our history and our heritage. The accountability we have here is better than anywhere else. When you live in a community like this, you know the guys that need help. You know the guys that you can depend on. You know the guys that are strong. You know the guys that are weak. We can't save them all. We can lead them to water, but we can't make them drink."[21]

As an aspiring young race car driver, Justin Allgaier remembers the late 1990s and early 2000s, when a number of high-profile drivers, such as Jeff Gordon and Dale Jarrett, were openly proclaiming their Christian faith. He was inspired by the public display, but also he was made aware of the platform's precarious nature.

"I remember some of the blunders that happened and some of the things that brought a negative light to [the faith movement]," Allgaier says. "That's something I've paid attention to and said, 'Okay, here's the things that I need to do.' You don't want to see anyone ever fail. I'm all for [sharing your faith]. But whether you're new to the faith or someone who's been around it your whole life, as long as you're trying to do better and you can admit your failures, that's the important thing to me."[22]

That's why unabashed accountability has been so important to Allgaier and his Bible study group, which includes Trevor Bayne, Michael McDowell, Ricky Stenhouse Jr., and Josh Wise, among others.

"They get together every week for Bible study," Cup series chaplain Stephen Keller says. "They share very honestly what they're struggling with, and they pray for each other. They see that they're not going to get condemned when they're honest about their struggles. They're experiencing grace as a reality through relationships and not just through vague concepts."23

Through the process with chaplains Clouse, Keller, and now Nick Terry, they have learned to more effectively deal with their humanity and embrace the concept of biblical grace as they carry the double-edged sword of high-profile Christianity.

"We've been inviting them to take a heart journey with God," Keller adds. "I've been saying to them all year, 'Don't focus on how bad you are.' Some Christians spend their whole lives focusing on their imperfections. But let's really get a glimpse of how good God is and embrace that. As we begin to do that, it's really going to change who we are. The transformation has got to be real, but I really do think they're beginning to get the message."24

As a seasoned veteran driver and committed Christian, David Reutimann admits that he is still figuring out how to deal with the raw emotions that so easily come out during the heat of battle. Life away from the track isn't exactly a cakewalk either.

"I stumble so much in everyday life," Reutimann confides. "It's still such a work in progress. I should be a lot further along, quite frankly, than I am in that respect. I've got more work to do on that side than I've ever had to do career-wise. Sometimes I just never seem to get it. It can be disheartening to see how bad you end up stumbling and saying things you shouldn't say and acting the way you shouldn't act."25

Because of his imperfections, Reutimann doesn't want anyone to look at him as the "picture of Christian faith in racing." That's not a cop-out but rather an honest self-assessment that helps him maintain a healthy level of humility.

"If there's a walking, talking picture of God's grace and his forgiveness and his tolerance for the stupidity of [humankind], I'm probably the poster child for that," Reutimann says. "I've been blessed in so many different ways, and a lot of times you say things or you act a certain way and you think, 'Man, I don't deserve any of this if I can't act better than that.' Sometimes it's a good reality check."[26]

Kurt Busch can relate. Much like his younger brother Kyle, 2011 wasn't exactly the best year of his NASCAR career. The season had a positive start with his first Budweiser Shootout victory in February and continued through the summer when he picked up a road course win at Infineon Raceway on June 26 in Sonoma, California. That same weekend, his relationship with girlfriend Patricia Driscoll was publically acknowledged for the first time.

But things turned sour in a hurry late in the season. Driving in Penske Racing's #22 car, Busch struggled mightily in the final five races. As his day ended early at the final race in Homestead, he lost patience with Dr. Jerry Punch, who was waiting for the signal from ESPN producers to conduct an interview. Busch ripped into Punch with a slew of profanities and later made an obscene gesture to workers as he tried to get past a car that was blocking his path to the garage area. Busch was officially released from Penske Racing on December 5.

It was a hard lesson for an emotionally charged driver who had already been working toward a greater understanding of God's role in his life.

"People forget that we're human, and we have bad days," Driscoll says. "They think we live this lifestyle of the rich and famous, and that we travel in private jets, and everything goes right for us all the time, when the truth is that we live life like normal people. We have normal lives, normal stresses, and it's ten times worse when you're living in a fishbowl and everybody gets to make a judgment for you. Kurt saw the pain that I was in. He saw the pain that [her son] Houston was in [during the custody battle]. That was a lot of stress for him too because he loves us both."[27]

For Busch and Driscoll, MRO was a safe haven of support and guidance throughout the roughest storms. In particular, they have become close friends with Monty and Melanie Self and Nick and Amy Terry. They also have a great deal of respect and love for Cup Chaplain Stephen Keller, from whom Busch particularly has found inspiration and encouraging words.

"You know, I think that Stephen is picking out Scriptures every week that have something to do with me," Busch once told Driscoll. "I think he knows what's going on, and he's always finding something relevant to us."[28]

According to Driscoll, MRO has been "a huge part" of helping Busch rediscover his faith.

"MRO has helped Kurt realize that he's not alone in the world," she says. "All of these people really do care, and they don't want anything from him. He's had so many people over the last ten years of his life, when he became famous, that just wanted something from him. You've got guys like Stephen and those guys that just care about our family and what's best for us. They've always been there to support us. There really are some good people out there, and they're right next to us."[29]

Undoubtedly, there are still some drivers, crew members, executives, and officials who see chapel service as a good-luck charm or perhaps as a way to ease the guilt that they might be carrying for their past transgressions. But Waltrip has another theory as to why several hundred people file in to participate in MRO's weekly time of worship and Bible devotion.

"For the most part, I think it's encouragement," he says. "If you're down and you're struggling, you need to hear the Word. If things are going well, you want to be sure that you're biblically doing what you should be doing. That's one thing that makes this community strong. It's how we do encourage each other, and how we do lift each other up, and how if there's tragedy, everybody rallies around each other. Spiritually, that really helps us all bond closer together."[30]

At the end of the day, however, the realization of one's mortality, whether it comes from an injury, a lost job, an illness in the family, or a failed marriage, can be a significant catalyst in helping push individuals toward a closer relationship with the Creator.

"You take all your problems to Christ, and that's your sounding board, that's your rock, that's everything," Kyle Petty says. "That's what faith is. It's that belief that there's Somebody there that's going to help you and push you and be that Person that's there for you when you're in your deepest, darkest moment. There's Somebody there that won't leave you alone. God is always standing by you. If you didn't believe that, then why would you even get out of bed every morning?"[31]

NOTES

1. Darrell Waltrip, interview with the author, October 2, 2010.
2. Dale Beaver, interview with the author, August 21, 2012.
3. Sam Hornish Jr., interview with the author, March 21, 2013.
4. Michael McDowell, interview with the author, October 1, 2010.
5. Ibid.
6. Ibid.
7. Jami McDowell, interview with the author, February 15, 2012.
8. Ibid.
9. Ashley Allgaier, interview with the author, January 17, 2012.
10. Ibid.
11. Matt Kenseth, interview with the author, November 1, 2008.
12. Darrell Waltrip, interview with the author, October 2, 2010.
13. Michael McDowell, interview with the author, October 1, 2010.
14. Jami McDowell, interview with the author, February 15, 2012.
15. Andy Petree, interview with the author, October 18, 2011.
16. Ibid.
17. Dale Beaver, interview with the author, August 21, 2012.
18. Dr. Jerry Punch, interview with the author, October 8, 2011.
19. Billy Mauldin, interview with the author, December 5, 2011.
20. Sam Hornish Jr., interview with the author, March 21, 2013.

21. Darrell Waltrip, interview with the author, October 2, 2010.
22. Justin Allgaier, interview with the author, January 17, 2012.

23. Stephen Keller, interview with the author, October 9, 2011.
24. Ibid.
25. David Reutimann, interview with the author, October 8, 2011.
26. Ibid.
27. Patricia Driscoll, interview with the author, September 29, 2012.
28. Ibid.
29. Ibid.
30. Darrell Waltrip, interview with the author, October 2, 2010.
31. Kyle Petty, interview with the author, June 30, 2011.

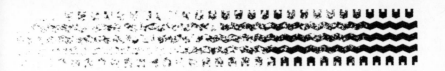

CHAPTER 14

The More Things Change

Stock car racing has advanced light years since its inception back in the late 1930s and throughout the 1940s, when moonshiners gathered at Daytona Beach to race on the Florida sand. NASCAR has gone from a weekend hobby to a $3 billion sport.

Because of that growth, many elements within the sport have experienced drastic changes. For instance, since the 1960s the NASCAR traveling community has increased from about five hundred people to over three thousand participants. Crews once consisted of two or three people. In some cases, individual drivers served as one-person crews, changing their own tires and fueling their own tank. But now a team's nucleus consists of a crew chief, a spotter, and a seven-member pit crew that features a jack man, a gas man, two tire changers, two tire carriers, and a utility man.

Some of NASCAR's biggest modifications have revolved around the sport's key ingredient: the cars. Once known for its strictly stock frame and body, the race car has gone through at least five distinct changes since 1948, including the highly modified bodies of the 1990s and early 2000s and the so-called Gen-6 car, which in some ways has completed the circle back to more of a showroom style, but with the latest high-tech safety elements.

And that's just scratching the surface of change that's taken place within NASCAR over the last sixty-plus years.

Much is also made of NASCAR's unique fan base. The stereo-types are pervasive and have been difficult to shake. When Cup series chaplain Stephen Keller joined Motor Racing Outreach (MRO) in 2010, he was fully aware of what the outside world gen-erally thought about stock car racing enthusiasts. Not that Keller had ever bought into those generalizations, but he did quickly learn for himself the truth of the matter.

"The media stereotype is that the NASCAR fan base is made up of low-income adults who probably haven't graduated from junior high school," Keller says. "It's a ridiculous stereotype. I've found a real intelligent fan base—folks who are really warm and are just fanatical about the sport. They spend their whole vacations out here just following us around."[1]

Statistics back up Keller's nonscientific observations. According to NASCAR's Fan Base Demographic study, just over 50 percent of NASCAR fans earn $50,000 or more, roughly 20 percent are minorities, almost 40 percent are female, and the geographic rep-resentation is very similar to the U.S. population. In other words, it's not just a Southern sport supported by white, blue-collar men.[2]

NASCAR has stepped up its efforts in recent years to diversify the demographics of its driving talent as well as its fan base. In 2004 the Drive for Diversity program was created in an attempt to bring more minorities and women into the sport, not just as drivers but also as executives and crew members. Some of the more notable products include drivers Kyle Larson (who is Japanese American) and Darrell Wallace Jr. (who is African American).

Even before the program was instituted, a stream of internation-al drivers were making their way to NASCAR from other racing disciplines. The list of notable imports has swelled to include Juan Pablo Montoya (Columbia), Marcos Ambrose (Australia), Max Papis (Italy), Nelson Piquet Jr. (Brazil), Juan Carlos Blum (Mexico), Dexter Stacey (Canada), and Miguel Paludo (Brazil), among others.

The influx of drivers from outside the traditional NASCAR belt-way has made for an interesting ministry dynamic.

"When you talk about people coming in from different backgrounds, you're tempted to start trying to stay relevant," MRO president Billy Mauldin says. "From a ministry standpoint, you end up chasing rabbit after rabbit. You can't really be culturally relevant to everybody when you have such a diverse community like this. It's impossible. You can't hire enough people that are reflective of the diversity that exists within the sport today. But Christ is always relevant. So as long as you stay consistent and Christlike in your service, it crosses all boundaries. So it doesn't matter if someone is coming into the sport from South America or Australia or South Africa or southern California or northern Maine. If you just stay consistent, then God meets them where they are."[3]

NASCAR has also been on the forefront of gender equity. In a sport in which women were once not even allowed to be in the pit area, the gap has dramatically closed thanks to the presence of drivers such as Danica Patrick, Chrissy Wallace, and Johanna Long, not to mention a slew of female publicists, NASCAR officials, media members, and track workers. Christmas Abbott made history in 2013 when she joined Michael Waltrip Racing to become the first full-time female crew member.

"There are a lot of women who pull for Danica Patrick, there are Colombians who pull for Juan Pablo Montoya, and there are Cubans who pull for Aric Almirola," Kyle Busch tells the *Richmond Times-Dispatch*. "That widens out our fan base. This is an American-made sport. It's been a Southeastern sport, and to be able to get diverse fans is great."[4]

Committed to Prayer

One thing that hasn't changed is the sport's commitment to faith in the public square. Ever since Rev. Hal Marchman first prayed on the PA system during the pre-race ceremonies at the 1959 Daytona 500, it has become standard procedure for the stock car community to ask God to bless the day's activities.

NASCAR has held firm despite the fact that prayers of invocation at public sporting events have become a rarity. Most public schools no longer allow prayer at high school football games or similar gatherings due to a 2000 ruling by the U.S. Supreme Court that the Establishment Clause in the First Amendment of the Constitution provided that the government (or government-run operations such as public school districts) may not establish a religion. Public universities such as the University of Tennessee have come under fire for refusing to stop the practice of prayer at football games.

In fact, NASCAR is the only professional sport that makes formal, public prayer a part of every event. There are a handful of exceptions, such as the Oklahoma City Thunder, which, as of the 2013 season, was the only NBA team to give a public invocation as part of its pre-game ceremonies.

Mauldin believes that NASCAR's commitment to public prayer and other expressions of faith is a direct reflection of its ardent supporters.

"Faith is a part of who the fans are," he says. "You wouldn't take away an invocation or a moment to recognize God from a group of people when that's who they are. They're all over the spectrum about how passionately they believe, but we're at the very least a country that has a sense of the importance of honoring God."[5]

For driver Blake Koch, there's a much bigger purpose behind the pre-race prayer, and that drives his desire to see it continue well into the future.

"Who knows how many people are affected by each of those prayers?" he wonders. "There might be a hundred thousand people out there in the stands. What if ten thousand people are deeply affected by that prayer and are reminded of God's presence and go to church the next week? Or even if they don't go to church, what if they just say a simple prayer that night? It's such an effective ministry tool."[6]

Committed to Ministry

Behind the scenes, NASCAR has supported track ministry in one form or another since Brother Bill Frazier pioneered the sport's chaplaincy efforts in 1970. NASCAR isn't unique in that regard. Major League Baseball receives Sunday ministry via Baseball Chapel. Most NFL teams have a chapel service the night before or the morning of their games. The PGA hosts public chapel services at many of its tournaments, including the Masters, and the NBA holds joint pre-game services for both teams.

The difference is that on-site ministry in NASCAR's arena is much more visible, whereas the other sports organizations' efforts tend to be more private in nature. Brad Daugherty has participated in ministry as an NBA star, a NASCAR analyst for ESPN, and a team owner with JTG Daugherty Racing.

"You've got a mobile operation in MRO that works throughout the motor sports industry," he explains. "They create a presence that's a little more available to everyone and especially for people to see. You've got every team in the sport at an event each weekend. Everyone in basketball, however, is all over the country. I played basketball in Cleveland, and we had Athletes in Action. We had a strong faith-based operation that supported our individual team. Each team had those. I think NASCAR is just different as opposed to more open. It's the way the sport operates and the way the venues operate that lends itself to people being able to stumble upon it or witness the interactions. That's the difference. I don't think [the presence of faith is] any more or less. I just think it's applied differently."[7]

Keller thinks about NASCAR's unique reality often. He's still amazed that MRO has such freedom to move about the garage area and pit road and the motor coach lot.

"Maybe it's because of its Southern roots," Keller says. "Maybe it's because there are a few of the NASCAR moms that would kill the leadership if they got rid of us."[8]

And maybe it's something else, such as MRO's careful attention to nondenominational ministry.

"That helps," Keller says. "We keep the services Protestant, but we also have a number of Roman Catholics that are at home with us. It's not mass, but we talk about Christ. We don't talk about the saints, but we still talk about the Scriptures. If anything, we suffer from association. Typically, people take their time [before deciding to attend] chapel or getting close to MRO. They're afraid that we are like the church where they had a bad experience. So when they find out that we don't represent a particular church, they realize we're here to encourage them in faith in general and to help them know God without trying to connect them to some church. That's when they begin to relax."

"A lot of those religious hang-ups in society fall away here," he continues. "It really doesn't matter where you come from. It's just Who you believe in and Who you're following. As Baptists, Methodists, or Roman Catholics, we find ourselves in a place where we can encourage one another in the Lord, and [denominationalism] never comes up. It's not a part of the conversation. All of those dividing walls have fallen down here."[9]

Darrell Waltrip adds that MRO's longevity has been fueled by its low-key nature and ability to stay out of the spotlight.

"We're not out here beating on doors, toting our Bibles around," he says. "We're very laid-back. We're here, and everybody knows we're here, and if you need us, that's what we're here for. But we're not out promoting. We try to blend in. We're not here to make a 'look at us' statement. We never have been. That's never been who we are, because we do understand and we do appreciate the fact that we're able to mingle in the garage and do what we do without a lot of problems."[10]

But ultimately, NASCAR embraces ministry at the track because it recognizes how much the racing community desires it.

"Most of these guys, from the lowest mechanic down the line up to the highest NASCAR official, have been aware of Christianity," NASCAR Hall of Fame driver Bobby Allison says. "They have had some recognition of Christianity in their life. They feel like this has helped from the beginning, and it's grown and grown. It's continued to help people. Everybody supports it because the one thing we have in common is the love of Jesus Christ."[11]

Resisting Political Correctness

Social activist groups have been monitoring and litigating civil rights cases for much of the twentieth century and beyond. The American Civil Liberties Union (ACLU), for example, has focused on issues such as freedom of speech and separation of church and state since it was founded in 1920. Because NASCAR is a privately owned entity, it has avoided much of the scrutiny that is typically aimed at government agencies and publically funded organizations.

This doesn't mean that NASCAR is exempt from future challenges as it pertains to its support of public prayer and, to a lesser degree, on-site ministry. And if its faith-based mentality is ever seriously tested, Buz McKim believes that the organization would be ready to go the distance.

"[NASCAR] would go head to head with someone like the ACLU," he says. "This is our deal. This is our thing. Go ahead and knock yourself out, but we're the eight-hundred-pound gorilla. We've got deep pockets, and we'll run it this way until the end."[12]

For the time being, there doesn't seem to be any indication that anything is changing anytime soon, especially not just for the sake of so-called political correctness or fitting in with the mainstream of professional sports.

"Faith has been a part of the sport from its earliest days," Kyle Petty says. "Once that's in your DNA, you don't pass an ordinance or pass a law or all of a sudden change your DNA. I don't think NASCAR can change its DNA. I think it's passed on from one generation to the next. The fans expect it. The drivers expect it. And more importantly, I think we all want it. I don't think they'll ever be able to rule it out."13

NASCAR historian Bryant McMurray believes that the key lies with the fans because NASCAR knows that they're the ones who control the purse strings to its financial success.

"As long as the moral fiber of the fan dictates the practice, it'll stay," he says. "If the moral fiber of the fan changes, then it definitely changes. This is entertainment. It is a show put on every week for a group of people every week fit to their desires. The fans will dictate to the sport what happens. But as long as the sport keeps the same business model of playing the national anthem and praying before the start of the race, there doesn't seem to be any downside to it."14

The fans certainly proved McMurray's theory true during the 2002 season. At the Truck Series race at Martinsville on April 13, an unnamed NASCAR official asked Morgan Shepherd to remove the Jesus decal from the hood of his unsponsored #21 car. Shepherd complied, but after NASCAR received many emails and phone calls from fans demanding a reversal of that decision, NASCAR did in fact allow Shepherd to put the logo back on the car—something he has continued to do ever since.15

And as far as Waltrip is concerned, the thought of certain traditions such as the pre-race prayer ever going away couldn't be further from his mind.

"I don't know why it would become a problem unless somebody just wanted to create a problem," he says. "Most people just realize that this is who we are. That's what I like about our sport and our leadership. If you don't like it, don't come. This is what we do. This is the way we race. This is the way we officiate. This is the way the sport is run. This is who we are, and if you want to be a part of it, we're glad to have you and we want to have you. But don't try to come in here trying to change us."[16]

The Grand National Paradox

For many of the sport's faithful believers, the vehement resistance of political correctness and the hopeful trust that NASCAR will never abandon its support of Christian ministry and public prayer are undoubtedly rooted in a sincere desire to maintain the unique opportunities to share the gospel on an enormous national platform. But for the sport's traditionalists, the motivation is just as likely to stem from a long history of resistance to outside social and political influence akin to the spirit displayed by the feisty, churchgoing Scots-Irish whose rebellious moonshine-running ways laid the groundwork for the birth of stock car racing.

It is in fact the paradoxical nature of the Scots-Irish that has continued throughout the history of NASCAR and remains today. Even as faith pioneers such as Hershel McGriff, Ned Jarrett, and Rev. Hal Marchman were blazing a trail for Christian influence within the sport, NASCAR was riddled with undertones of racism, sexism, and immoral behavior that routinely included heavy drinking, brawling, and widespread adultery.

NASCAR has made great strides, particularly during the early twenty-first century, to increase diversity and neutralize chauvinism through intentional programs and education. As documented earlier in this chapter, there are more women and a larger percentage of minorities involved at all levels. Lesa France Kennedy, executive vice president of NASCAR, and Marcus Jadotte, vice president of public affairs, provide two powerful examples of this continuing paradigm shift.

Even so, NASCAR still has a long way to go before completely eradicating all elements of its unsavory past. Because of that, just like in the sport's earliest days, the paradox between authentic faith expression and secular influence is still very much alive, if not in different forms. For instance, although tobacco products have not been affiliated with NASCAR since 2010, alcoholic beverage companies continue to have a pervasive presence via advertisements and team sponsorships. And although some of the rabble-rousing that marred the sport's image early on has been significantly reduced, issues such as marital and family strife and drug and alcohol use touch NASCAR lives, just like everywhere else in today's society.

In other words, Darrell Waltrip was right when he described NASCAR as an "unsanitized environment."

"There's nothing pretentious about this crowd," he says. "Not at all. What you see is what you get. There are a lot of guys out here that are strong believers, but they still smoke and drink and like to have a good time. No one out here is perfect."[17]

In that regard, the NASCAR community, while in some ways vastly different, is at its core really the same as any other group of people in the United States. All of us wrestle with imperfections, hypocrisies, and impure motives. And all of us need a Savior. No matter what changes come our way and what pressures squeeze against us, that is one fact that will never change.

And for people such as Billy Mauldin, it's the reason he shows up to work every day with the hope that one imperfect soul might be able to help other imperfect souls find their way to the Truth.

"NASCAR provides one of the most unique ministry opportunities out there," he says. "But if you feel like you're going to get people saved, you're kidding yourself. You've overinflated your ego a little bit. All you can ask for is for someone to listen to you. You can't make them make a decision. That's the work of the Holy Spirit. If you can earn people's trust and respect and their willingness to listen to you, or just get them to observe you and then just be Christ to them, you've created an atmosphere and an arena where God can set the stage for the Holy Spirit to do what only He can do."[18]

NOTES

1. Stephen Keller, interview with the author, October 9, 2011.
2. "NASCAR Fan Base Demographics," 2012 (https://s3.amazonaws.com/nascarassets/assets/1/page/2012%20nascar%20fan%20base%20demographics.pdf).
3. Billy Mauldin, interview with the author, December 5, 2011.
4. Louis Llovio, "Diversity Makes Inroads in NASCAR," *Richmond Times-Dispatch*, April 22, 2013.
5. Billy Mauldin, interview with the author, December 5, 2011.
6. Blake Koch, interview with the author, October 8, 2011.
7. Brad Daugherty, interview with the author, October 1, 2010.
8. Stephen Keller, interview with the author, October 9, 2011.
9. Ibid.
10. Darrell Waltrip, interview with the author, October 2, 2010.
11. Bobby Allison, interview with the author, February 14, 2012.
12. Buz McKim, interview with the author, January 31, 2012.
13. Kyle Petty, interview with the author, June 30, 2011.
14. Bryant McMurray, interview with the author, September 17, 2012.
15. RacingWest.com, "Morgan Shepherd's Jesus Logo…NASCAR Says Yes!" July 10, 2002 (http://www.racingwest.com/news/articles/4484-morgan-shepherds-jesus-logo-nascar-says-yes.html).
16. Darrell Waltrip, interview with the author, October 2, 2010.
17. Ibid.
18. Billy Mauldin, interview with the author, December 5, 2011.

Afterword

For a number of years now, I have stood on pit wall at Homestead Miami Speedway and watched the final laps unwind in the last race of the NASCAR Sprint Cup series. For me, it has become somewhat of a tradition that I have shared with other Motor Racing Outreach (MRO) chaplains over the years. At that moment, you have the opportunity to watch two incredible celebrations begin to unfold.

First, you witness the exultation of the winner of the race, the final race of the season, which every team would like to win in order to see their season end on a high note. The victorious team also embraces it as an opportunity to take momentum into the upcoming season, which will kick off in just a couple months. From my viewing point atop the pit wall, I can watch the entire celebration taking place in Victory Lane: high-fives, champagne, fireworks, interviews with radio and television reporters, and, of course, what seems like a never-ending process of photographs. Everyone is excited and thrilled.

From the same vantage point, I can spin 180 degrees and see the start-finish line. It is there that another stage has been set up as soon as the race concluded, and it is from this stage that a second celebration takes place, crowning the year's champion in NASCAR's premier division, its Sprint Cup series.

On this stage the celebration is in many ways similar to the one taking place in Victory Lane, only the champion for the season has a little more to celebrate. The winning driver and team have accomplished, as a group, what every competitor in stock car racing dreams of doing: becoming a NASCAR Sprint Cup Champion. This celebration is about the relief that everyone on the team feels in accomplishing the goal. For many, whether driver, crew member, team owner, or family member, a lifelong dream has finally been realized.

For two teams (because the celebrations almost always feature two different competitors), it is a great night—celebration, excitement, and a level of satisfaction that will take them through the coming days and weeks as they prepare for another season of racing, which is just around the corner. But for forty other teams, that night is another story.

From my vantage point on the pit wall, I can jump down and walk about twenty-five yards and be inside the NASCAR garage. For the teams that did not win the race, and for those who did not win a championship, it is another experience entirely. For them, it is all about one thing: packing up and getting out of Homestead as soon as possible.

For many of the teams, the night becomes focused on returning home and starting to prepare for the upcoming season, or getting home and getting ready for the Thanksgiving holiday. Finally, they will be able to spend some much-needed time with family and friends. At last, they will get to rest up from what has been a long season for everyone. While two great celebrations go on trackside, back in the garage, in about thirty minutes or less, almost every team has packed up their haulers, their gear, and the cars they raced, and they are heading out to the airports. In a matter of minutes, the garage has gone from a hustling, bustling workplace to what essentially looks like a vacant parking lot. Just twenty-five yards apart, there are two different worlds, and as a chaplain, I have the unique opportunity to walk in both of these worlds.

What has often caught my eye on that final race night is one particular moment that I witness every year, and it is the same both for those who celebrate this night and for those who just want the night to end. It is the scene I witness every year of the lone person walking off the track, out of the garage, back to their car. With everything that is going on, it is easy to miss them, but without exception there is always one. It is in this moment that I am reminded regularly of what Jesus Christ did for me over two decades ago and has done for many, many more people over the history of humankind.

There was a time in my life when I was the one who walked for a season in a very lonely place. I was not physically alone. A wonderful family and great friends surrounded me. What I did not have, though, was a real relationship with Jesus, and I did not know God, my heavenly Father. Like those I watch in Homestead, I was busy with life, working and doing, just as so many others are working and doing. Yet inside, something was desperately missing that left me empty in a way I could not explain. Then one morning, in a construction trailer on a job site in Savannah, Georgia, I knelt down on a dusty floor and said these simple words: "God, I am tired of hurting. If you can do anything, please help."

That was it. That was all I said. That was my profound prayer. But I can tell you this: I got up off my knees and walked to the door to go outside, and when I hit the top step, I realized something that I needed desperately at that moment. I knew I was not alone. I knew I was no longer a solitary person walking through and out of the "garage" of life. Something was different, and no one new was physically in my life. Something was different, and it was Jesus. He had come to be with me, and I knew it.

I share this with you because I see the same thing take place in the lives of men and women everywhere. On any given day I can look to my left and see those who seem to be celebrating and enjoying life. Then I turn and look to my right and see those who are just doing what it takes to get it done. Nothing is necessarily wrong with either activity on the surface, until you come to realize that both the highs and the lows of life are intended to be experienced with God at the center of our lives. We were created first and foremost to be in a personal relationship with the Lord. We were created to live and walk through life with our Creator. God becomes our unseen joy and strength when all that can be seen does nothing for us. The Lord shows us true, unconditional love when the world that we live in most often demands something from us, something in exchange for its love and attention.

Where are you today? Are you celebrating a big win? Maybe even a championship in your life? Or are you struggling to just make sense of the world you live in? Are you going through the motions, surrounded by thousands yet also lonely and struggling to find purpose? I promise you: if you will find your own quiet spot and simply do as I did, ask God to help you, then Jesus will show up. I offer you no fancy prayer to repeat after me, but only encouragement to be yourself and share with God what you think or feel right now. God is there. God is listening. God hears your prayers.

Another season will come and go in NASCAR. Another champion will be crowned, and more races will be won. Highs and lows will be experienced by everyone once again, but what about you? Is today your day to start a "new season" of life? Is today your day to begin a life where you personally know the Creator of the universe? Standing on top of a heavenly pit wall, God is watching over us all. The Lord also steps down and walks through the "garage" of our lives. God sees us celebrating and struggling, and in both cases the Lord just wants to walk through it with us. The choice is yours. Invite Jesus to join you today. In your own simple and real way, pray, and Jesus will meet you at the top step, just as he met me.

—Billy Mauldin
President and CEO
Motor Racing Outreach